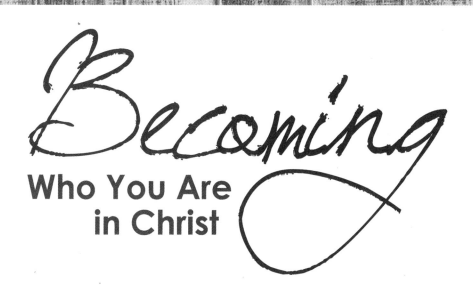

Becoming
Who You Are
in Christ

D0913327

Loveland, Colorado

Group resources actually work!

This Group resource incorporates our R.E.A.L. approach to ministry. It reinforces a growing friendship with Jesus, encourages long-term learning, and results in life transformation, because it's

Relational
Learner-to-learner interaction enhances learning and builds Christian friendships.

Experiential
What learners experience through discussion and action sticks with them up to 9 times longer than what they simply hear or read.

Applicable
The aim of Christian education is to equip learners to be both hearers and doers of God's Word.

Learner-based
Learners understand and retain more when the learning process takes into consideration how they learn best.

Visit our websites: **group.com** and **group.com/women**

This resource is brought to you by the wildly creative women's ministry team at Group. Choose Group resources for your women's ministry and experience the difference!

Unless otherwise indicated, all Scripture quotations are taken from the *Holy Bible*, New Living Translation®, copyright © 1996, 2004. Used by permission of Tyndale House Publishers, Inc., Carol Stream, Illinois 60188. All rights reserved.

ISBN 978-0-7644-7820-8

Printed in the United States of America.

10 9 8 7 6 5   21 20 19 18 17 16

Contents

Introduction

"I praise you because I am fearfully and wonderfully made; your works are wonderful, I know that full well." (Psalm 139:14)

Welcome to Wonderfully Made, a movement of girls and women like you who are passionate about living lives of lasting value, beauty, and purpose.

Maybe you're holding this book and wondering how in the world you got it. Maybe you're not sure what you believe about God, about Jesus, about yourself, or about your place in this world. We just want to tell you that we're glad you're here. We understand you because we've been where you are—and we're the first to admit that we still don't have it all figured out. We've questioned who we are, who we're supposed to be, and why we are here. We've struggled to make sense of this crazy world. We've wrestled with our faith.

We believe the answer to these questions begins with one simple, mysterious, and profound truth: you have been made. Made by God and made for a purpose. You are not an accident. Your life is not the result of random chance. You have been beautifully, lovingly, and marvelously created. You exist because of God and for God. Not only were you created by God but you were created for a relationship with God. And that relationship is possible through Jesus Christ.

How do you answer the question *Who are you?* There are so many different roles we can play and so many masks we can wear. Our identity is often shaped by our surroundings and experiences. However, those masks we put on are not truly who we are—they are false and temporary. True identity comes from the One who made us, and that's what we'll explore together though this study.

We invite you to take a journey with us, one of discovering who God is, the kind of woman he created you to be, and the life he has for you. *Wonderfully Made: Becoming Who You Are in Christ* is a guidebook to understanding your true identity in Christ. When we firmly establish our identity in Christ and choose to believe what God says about us is true, something amazing happens. We no longer have to worry about "finding ourselves" or "creating ourselves" because we understand that in Christ we have been found.

Our hope is that through this journey, you will

- Be inspired, encouraged, and challenged to know your true value.

- Begin, grow, or deepen your relationship with God.

- Be empowered to live an outward-focused life and make a difference.

- Have fun on this journey called life as you step into your true identity.

We are so glad you are here. We invite you to learn more about our community of women and get more involved at wonderfullymade.org.

Love & Hugs,

The Wonderfully Made Team

Allie   Natalie

Kayla   Christie

wonderfullymade®
♥know your value

Allie Marie Smith | Kayla Mertes | Natalie Lynn Borton | Christie Myers

How to Use This Book

We encourage you to work through each lesson at your own pace. We've found it works great to spread the personal study out over the week, giving you plenty of time to absorb the material and not feel rushed or overwhelmed. The reason we didn't give you specific homework for specific days is so that you can do the lessons in the way that works best for you. Please don't feel pressured to do the a lesson in one sitting, but rather make a commitment to be intentional with your study by setting aside a little bit of time each day. To help the truths sink in deeply, we recommend having a Bible and journal handy as you dive into each week's lesson.

This study is designed to be done in a small group of four to ten girls or women. Each lesson includes both a personal study section (that you do yourself) and a group study outline (that you do with others). This book can also be used individually if you desire; however, we've found that going through it with at least one other person offers valuable encouragement and community.

If you have a larger group using this resource together, we encourage you to break into smaller groups during your weekly meetings. There are six lessons total; it's up to your group to decide if you'd like to do the study in six weeks or spread it out across twelve weeks. Choose whatever works best for your group's schedules and needs.

When you get together with others for the group portion, we recommend having one or two facilitators, depending on the size of your group. Feel free to break into smaller groups, if needed, to make the sharing time more personal. Each girl needs her own copy of this book so she can journal in it and make it her own!

Friendship and community is a core part of any Wonderfully Made group. Our hope is that you embrace this gift wholeheartedly. Be the friend, listener, and encourager you would want for yourself. We ask that you treat your sisters as you'd like to be treated—with respect and keeping confidential all the information that's shared. Our desire is that this will be a place where you feel welcome, safe, and valued.

We're so excited that you're a part of Wonderfully Made and pray that God will shine his face upon your journey toward becoming the woman he created you to be!

ONE: *Discovering Your Value*
Personal Study

"When a woman knows that she is loved and loved deeply, she glows from the inside. This radiance stems from a heart that has had its deepest questions answered. 'Am I lovely? Am I worth fighting for? Have I been and will I continue to be romanced?' When these questions are answered, yes, a restful quiet spirit settles in a woman's heart."[1]
(John and Stasi Eldredge)

Hidden deep within the heart of every girl lies a series of lingering questions:

Am I worthy?

Am I enough?

Do you think I'm beautiful?

Am I of value—to my friends, my family, and the world?

From girlhood to womanhood, we are on a quest to have these questions answered with a resounding "yes!" The desire to be found worthy, loved, beautiful, and valuable is an insatiable search for significance, a soul hunger that fuels our every dream, decision, and relationship. Our search for value is unbreakably tied to our self-identity—how we perceive ourselves.

How do you answer the question, "Who are you?"

Are you your name?

Your parents' daughter?

Your boyfriend's girlfriend?

Are you your sport, job, GPA, talent, or checking account balance?

Are you an accumulation of all these things put together?

Take some time to reflect on who you are, and write your thoughts here.

My reflections: _____

_____

_____

_____

_____

_____

There are limitless roles, material things, and identities you can "put on" to give you a sense of value. You can wear the role of an exceptional student, a great athlete, the nice girl, the successful working girl, or so-and-so's girlfriend. Dressing ourselves in desirable roles, lofty achievements, fashionable clothes, and coveted appearances seems like the best strategy to silence the pervading insecurities we face. However, these roles, identities, and masks offer a sense of significance that only temporarily hides the frail inadequacies within our hearts.

While our relationships, interests, talents, and roles converge to give us a sense of self-worth, there's a much more pressing identity issue our souls won't let us ignore. We ache to know our core identity: where we came from, why we exist, what we're worth, and who we really are. Unless you choose to totally ignore humanity's most pressing question, you must either believe that we inexplicably "just happened" and evolved or that we were divinely created by God. Ultimately, our worldview shapes our identity-view, and what we believe about our origin dictates how we understand ourselves and our value.

This study you're working through now builds on a foundational belief in the God of the Bible (the bestselling book of all time). Romans 1:20 says, "For ever since the world was created, people have seen the earth and sky. Through everything God made, they can clearly see his invisible qualities—his eternal power and divine nature. So they have no excuse for not knowing God."

While creation gives evidence for God, Jesus is the exact representation of the Creator (Hebrews 1:3). We stand on the belief that Jesus Christ is who he said he is as recorded in the New Testament. This is what we mean by "discovering who we are in Christ." It's the journey of knowing Jesus and discovering our part in his story. In God, "we live and move and exist" (Acts 17:28), so it is only fitting that through him we discover our true identity, purpose, and worth.

I was a good girl from a good home. I was a tomboy with missing front teeth who loved to play dress up in my mom's pearls and high heels. I had a freckled face that turned tomato red after my soccer games, and I was as feisty as a girl could be. Sometime between growing from a girl into a young woman, my happiness, stubbornness, and confidence began to fade, and by the age of 12, feelings of unexplained sadness and unworthiness came to visit me.

Allie's Story

I started attending an all-girls private high school with everything going for me. On the outside, my life looked picture-perfect. I got straight A's, was captain of the soccer team, dated the captain of the football team from the all-boys school, and was well liked and accepted by my popular group of friends. But under the surface, I was crumbling with self-doubt, loneliness, and insecurity. During my sophomore year, the guy I was dating dumped me for one of my close friends. This broke my heart and seemed to confirm the lies I already believed about myself—that I wasn't pretty enough or skinny enough and that I didn't have a good personality.

Throughout high school I continued to battle insecurity, poor body image, and disordered eating. On the drive home from Friday night parties or football games, I often felt the urge to crash my blue Ford Explorer against the concrete on-ramp. I longed for an escape from the endless striving and sense of unworthiness and sadness. I tried hard to make myself happy and valuable. Next to my white nightstand sat my stack of self-help books and the journal where I confided my deepest thoughts and listed my big, lofty goals: to lose 10 pounds; to get a full-ride scholarship for soccer; to be a model. I believed once I looked a certain way, started school at my ideal college, and achieved notable accomplishments, I would be happy, worthy, and loved.

Shortly after I graduated summa cum laude from high school, I came undone. A dangerous combination of physiological, hormonal, emotional, and spiritual circumstances culminated in a deep, debilitating depression, and I found myself unable to sleep, talk, or eat. My body was alive, but there was no life within me. I remember lying on my bedroom floor with the lights off, the shades drawn, the light in my eyes dark, and the smile on my face hidden. Three weeks after graduation, I found myself in the behavioral health section of the hospital, signing papers saying that I was a danger to myself. Everything that had deemed me worthy in the world's eyes was stripped from me. My success. My beauty. My dreams. My goals. Even my sanity.

God began to use Christians in my family's life to shine light in my darkness. They began praying for me, offering me verses and words of encouragement. I became hungry to intimately know the God of the Bible whom I always believed in, and I threw myself into a relationship with him that would forever change me. As everything I claimed to be and placed my self-worth in was stripped from me, I was free to allow God to clothe me in my new identity. As I allowed Jesus to heal the innermost parts of me, I began to build my value and worth in him—simply as his daughter.

In Search of Value

Today's generation of girls and young women are having a hard time believing their value. We are people who don't what it means to be "wonderfully made."

- Only 4% of women describe themselves as beautiful.[2]

- Up to 20% of girls ages 10 to 19 are experiencing episodes of major depression.[3]
- Roughly 1 in 3 women will have an abortion.[4]

- 1 in 4 women will be sexually abused before the age of 18.[5]

- As many as 10 million girls and women are fighting a life-and-death battle with an eating disorder such as anorexia or bulimia.[6]

- In 2005, about one-tenth of all teenage girls tried to end their lives.[7]

- The prevalence of self-injury among teenage girls and young women is rising dramatically.[8]

The world's solution to insecurity is to simply find inner strength and love yourself. In the September 2009 issue of Glamour Magazine, Jessica Simpson opened up about her lifelong struggle with self-confidence and body image: "No matter how much money you spend to make yourself beautiful—with all the products, the diets, the plastic surgery—in the end, women need to fall in love with themselves and realize they're beautifully and wonderfully made."[9]

We commend Jessica Simpson and other celebrities for offering wisdom and opening up about their struggles. We totally agree that women need to know they are beautifully and wonderfully made. As a ministry, we are obsessed with spreading this message to women everywhere, but the very last thing we need to do is try to fall in love with ourselves. It doesn't work. We have tried, and failed. Failed miserably.

As warm-fuzzy, promising, and hopeful as the words of the world may sound, the world is never going to tell you the full truth. The truth is, you haven't been wired to fall in love with yourself but have been created to fall in love with the One who made you. Through knowing and loving our Maker, we will discover our true value. We can then love others and even ourselves because God first loved us.

There's a deeper message behind being wonderfully made that no "real beauty" campaign, celebrity, or any other self-esteem movement the world promotes is going to share. And it's this: You are not an accident. You have a Maker. A Maker who loves you, who knows you. Who calls you worthy. Beautiful. Valuable. A God who has planned all of your days before one of them came to be (Psalm 139:16). A Maker who has sent his Son, Jesus Christ, into this broken world to redeem you (John 3:16); to one day make things right; to turn your ashes into beauty (Isaiah 61:3); to give you a hope and a future (Jeremiah 29:11); and to give you life to the fullest (John 10:10) and life everlasting.

To be a girl who knows her worth requires that you look away from the world's value system and instead look into the Word of God. Because it's there we discover why we are here and who we really are.

Our True Value
Our true value isn't that we're beautiful, brilliant, talented, or fabulous. It is not hidden in what others think of us or what we think of ourselves. It is not equal to our output—our accolades, failures, or potential.

The truth is, we are but a vapor, here today and gone tomorrow (James 4:14), yet God loves us. We are messed up, fragile, and coming apart at the seams, yet God doesn't abandon us.

We have worth because God himself is worthy and he calls us his own. "See how very much our Father loves us, for he calls us his children, and that is what we are" (1 John 3:1). We are worthy because our Maker and Life-Giver loves us in a way no friend, parent, boyfriend, husband, or person could ever match. God extravagantly, unconditionally, and boundlessly loves us.

Though we fall short, God picks us up. He sees us (you!) as worthy enough to fight for, die for, and to redeem. He has made a way for our wrongs to be forgotten and forgiven. For our sickness and sin and frailties to be healed and our souls to never perish. Our true value does not lie in who we are, but in who God is and in who we are as his children.

The Definition of Me
It's so natural to define ourselves in terms of our relationships, talents, hobbies, and accomplishments. Take some time to reflect on the specific things you define yourself by.

- What identity do you "clothe" yourself in each morning?

_____

_____

_____

- How do you want other people to perceive or define you? Is this important to you? Why or why not?

_____

_____

_____

• What ability, advantage, possession or relationship do you take the most pride in?

_____

_____

_____

You are not your job. You are not your best talent. You are not your failures or set-backs. Take time to reflect on the thoughts below, and write down the things you consciously or subconsciously define yourself by. Some ideas include your job, your relationships, your appearance, and your possessions. Let this exercise be a reminder of what your true identity is not.

I am not _____

I am not _____

I am not _____

I am not _____

I am not _____

Whatever we try to clothe ourselves in other than our identity in Christ is a mask, a temporary cover for the needs, hurts, and desires only God can fulfill.

Losing Yourself

On the journey toward self-discovery, how often do we hear people say something like this:

I just need to find myself.

I'm still figuring out who I really am.

Life isn't about finding yourself, it's about creating yourself.

Our true self cannot be found through writing poetry, meditative enlightenment, world travels, or deep introspection. A self-consuming hunt for your true self does not begin and end with you. We must lose ourselves to truly be found. Jesus tells us: "Whoever finds their life will lose it, and whoever loses their life for my sake will find it" (Matthew 10:39, NIV).

As author Eugene Lowry said, "The search for one's identity is doomed for failure because it rests on the false premise it is incumbent upon us to be successful in the search for self. Instead the gospel declares that we have been found; that identity is a gift one can never obtain or reach on the basis of human effort."[10]

In the same way that you don't need to find yourself or create your life, you don't need to worry about creating the "perfect personality." C.S. Lewis said, "The more we let God take us over, the more truly ourselves we become—

because He made us. He invented us... It is when I turn to Christ, when I give up myself to His personality, that I first begin to have a real personality of my own."

The more consumed we become by the character of God and the causes he cares about, the less consumed we become with trying to figure our whole life out. When we really love God with our whole heart, mind, and soul, our whole focus changes. Instead of trying to love or find ourselves or getting others to love us, we find that we are flawed, ordinary people, extravagantly loved by an extraordinary God. Our true value (not our value to the world) isn't dependent on what we do or don't do. Apart from our Maker, we are absolutely nothing.

How do I become God's daughter?
We invite you to turn to page 90 in the back of this study to learn how you can make the decision to commit your life to Christ if you haven't done so before.

Remember that your significance doesn't come from doing, but simply being. You are invited to receive the most amazing identity: daughter of God. You didn't do and can't do anything to deserve God's love. Through faith in Christ, you are adopted into God's family (John 1:12). Now, hold your head up high!

Prepare your heart before God. Quiet your spirit, and spend some moments in prayer.

Loving Father,

It is in you that I live and move and have my being. You are the author of my life, the perfecter and finisher of my faith. Help me let go of the things I have placed my value in and to cling tightly to my identity and worth as your daughter. Reveal yourself to me in a greater way as I seek to live a life of lasting beauty, purpose, and significance.

My reflections: _____

_____

_____

_____

_____

_____

_____

ONE: *Discovering Your Value*

Group Study

Settle In and Catch Up
Set aside 15 minutes to catch up on life before you dig into this week's study. Get to know each other better!

Recap
Discuss this past week's lesson. What resonated with you? What did God teach you?

Sharing and Discussion
Use these questions to go deeper in your sharing. Be sure everyone has a chance to talk. This might mean you need to form smaller groups or pairs. And remember, what is shared here is shared in confidence.

This week, you had an opportunity to reflect on and answer questions about *your* identity. Take time now to share with each other what you discovered:

- How do you define yourself to other people?

- What identity do you "clothe" yourself in each morning?

- How do you want other people to perceive or define you? Is this important to you? Why or why not?

- What ability, advantage, possession, or relationship do you take the most pride in?

Reflection
Play J.J. Heller's song "True Things." This is available through iTunes or can be found on YouTube. Take time to reflect on the lyrics in this song, and then share your thoughts. (You can hear more of J.J. Heller's music at jjheller.com.)

Now spend a few minutes sharing your personal "prayer of identity." Refer to your responses on pages 13 and 14.

Take about 5 minutes to respond to the following questions on your own. Record your thoughts in the space provided. Once you're finished, you'll have the opportunity to share your responses with the group. You may want to get into groups of four or into pairs for the time of sharing.

- What are some of the places and relationships girls look to for a reflection of their value?

_____

_____

_____

- What lies has the world told you about your value?

_____
_____
_____

- What is a time when you felt that you weren't "good enough"?

_____
_____
_____

- What worldly ways have you tried, hoping they would make you valuable, beautiful, or worthy? Explain whether you succeeded or failed.

_____
_____
_____

Prayer

Grab one other person in your group, exchange prayer requests, and spend a few minutes praying for one another.

Write prayer requests here: _____

_____
_____
_____
_____
_____
_____
_____
_____
_____
_____
_____

TWO: *Three Keys to True Confidence*
Personal Study

"The most beautiful women I've ever observed are those that have exchanged a self-focused life for a Christ-focused one. They are confident, but not in themselves. Instead of self-confidence, they radiate with Christ-confidence. They aren't spending their time trying to feel better about themselves or inhabiting their own beauty. They aren't even thinking about themselves. Their desire is to decrease, so that Jesus Christ would increase."[1] (Leslie Ludy)

"The Lord is my strength and shield. I trust him with all my heart. He helps me, and my heart is filled with joy." (Psalm 28:7)

Marilyn Monroe. Madonna. Lady Gaga. These are names we all know. They evoke strong images in our minds. Marilyn stands over a street vent, laughing mischievously as she lets the breeze blow up her sexy white dress. Madonna's looks have ranged from grunge to glam and back again, but her strong arms, in-your-face attitude, and pouty lips remain and have become the trademark of today's independent woman. She's almost a modern reinvention of Monroe, but she's a little less playful and much more fierce.

Then there's Lady Gaga. We don't know what to say about her, except that she's taken the whole actress-singer thing to a whole new level. It's as if she was born for the stage, and her crazy makeup and outrageous fashion have once again set an extreme standard for young women across the world. Her hair color seems to change on a weekly basis, and she wears black lipstick like it's pink. You can't help but rock your hips when you hear her dance songs. She kind of took Madonna's makings, erased any trace of Marilyn Monroe that was left in the script, and sprinkled in a gothic edge. The playful femininity is gone, but the sex is pumped up, and it's wearing black.

However much the image has changed over time, there are several qualities these iconic women share. Each marks the "new woman" of her era, puts a new brand on what it is to be sexy, and appears to be confident. Right? They used their talents to get to the top and achieved the dream of wealth, charm, and fame.

- How does culture seem to define confidence?

_____

_____

_____

_____

_____

_____

_____

_____

_____

Have you heard that old saying "The proof is in the pudding?" Not many of us eat pudding. We prefer frozen yogurt! But the point is that it's easy to see how well a recipe works by tasting the final product. Let's take a closer look at the life of Marilyn Monroe to see how well culture's recipe for confidence worked for her.

The real girl behind the glamour was named Norma Jeane Baker. Norma's birth mother was mentally incapable of caring for her. She spent years in countless foster homes, and later suffered three failed marriages. Alcoholism, affairs, and depression consumed this silver-screen beauty's life. But during her years of fame, millions of onlookers gazed at her from a distance and saw Marilyn Monroe—a sexy, confident star, full of life and charisma. Monroe's life culminated in a broken heart and a drug overdose at the age of 36. No amount of beauty, money, or men could satisfy her longing for love and acceptance or give her the confidence she needed to carry on. In the end, even her stubborn determination and survivor mentality failed her.

Monroe's plight is not the exception to the rule. Madonna is still turning out hit singles, setting fashion trends, and adorning the covers of major magazines, but she expresses an inner anxiety that she can't seem to shake. In one interview, Madonna shared, "I have an iron will, and all of my will has always been to conquer some horrible feeling of inadequacy...I push past one spell of it and discover myself as a special human being, and then I get to another stage and think I'm mediocre and uninteresting." Later in that interview, Madonna admits to the fear of mediocrity pushing her to prove herself and says this is a constant and ongoing struggle.

We applaud this woman's honesty. Each of us has experienced the struggle she's talking about, and many of us are still experiencing it. We're striving for a sense of inner satisfaction, peace, and significance that lasts. We want true confidence. But what we have is a knockoff version of it that leaves us unsatisfied and fearful of failure, rejection, or mediocrity. Even Lady Gaga— whom the media applauds for self-confidence and fearlessness—admits that she wakes up in the morning feeling insecure.

Clearly there's something wrong here! The recipe we see for "confidence" in magazines, movies, and music isn't working even for the women who advertise it. We're never going to attain confidence by trying to be beautiful enough or perform well enough or get enough attention. When it comes to these things, enough is never enough. The more we strive for them, the more unattainable they seem. We always think we'll be satisfied and feel good about ourselves with the next accomplishment, but when the novelty of that achievement wears off, we find ourselves right back where we started, doubting ourselves. It's a never-ending checklist. And we exhaust ourselves trying to meet the demands.

The problem for most of us is that we have bought into the lie that we're not good enough just as we are and not beautiful enough just as God made us. This has stirred up a deep discontentment within our hearts. And we're searching for a fix. Lies are constantly thrown at us by the world (culture, media, and sometimes other people), but they originate from the enemy (Satan). Listen to what Jesus says about Satan's tactics:

He was a murderer from the beginning. He has always hated the truth, because there is no truth in him. When he lies, it is consistent with his character; for he is a liar and the father of lies. (John 8:44)

When we feel discouraged, inadequate, or insecure, it is because we are buying into Satan's lies. Sometimes these lies can disguise themselves as our own thoughts or even integrate themselves into our patterns of thinking so that we don't recognize them anymore.

- Can you identify some of the lies (discouraging words or thoughts) you've believed about yourself? Write about them here.

_____

_____

_____

Here's the good news! There is a sure solution that will empower and enable us to crush the lies that make us feel like we'll never measure up. This solution is the truth, and it's found in the Word of God, the Bible. Jesus assures us, "And you will know the truth, and the truth will set you free" (John 8:32).

Satan knows that truth is the key to freedom, so he wants to keep us from knowing it and believing it. These are both necessary for freedom. We can't just know the truth, we have to believe it. But in order to believe it, we have to start by knowing it. That's why the Bible says "Faith comes from hearing, that is, hearing the Good News about Christ" (Romans 10:17).

Are you ready to dive into God's Word and be free? Are you ready for true confidence?

- What insecurities, anxieties, or fears do you want to break free from?

_____

_____

_____

Confidence comes from knowing who you are and being comfortable in that. I used to have a fake sense of confidence. I was a cheerleader, I was popular, I was blonde and perky, and I thought I was confident in that. But it was all false, and I was also unhappy. I carried that fake confidence with me to college, where I had an amazing group of women in my life who led me to Christ, and for the first time in my life, I began to have a true confidence in knowing who my Creator made me to be. My confidence comes from knowing that I am the bride of Christ, I have the most perfect Father, and I am so loved just as I am. I am always growing toward him and changing, but I never have to be a certain way to know who I am, and I can be confident in that.

Taylor's Story

God will set you free from these things if you put your trust in him. He is the ultimate Healer. There is nothing so deep and so dark that God cannot free us from it. Jesus says he holds the keys to death and hell because he triumphed over them when he died on the cross and rose from the dead. His death-conquering power is the power that is available to us when he is our Savior and King. All we have to do is ask. So let's start by opening ourselves up to the power of God in prayer.

Jesus,

Thank you that I can come to you for truth, healing, and transformation. Please reveal to me the lies I have believed about myself, and show me the truth about who I am because of your love. I ask that you would let me see myself as you see me, God, and that you would give me faith to believe your Word.

Okay, beautiful one, let's search God's Word and discover three keys of truth that will unlock the floodgates of true confidence into our hearts if we believe!

Key #1—Trust in God

Trust is a vital component of confidence because where we put our trust will determine the source of our confidence, and we need that source to be consistent, reliable, and capable of giving us the real deal.

Here are sections of the Bible that will transform your life if you take them to heart. To start, look up Psalm 121.

- What does this psalm tell you about the way God cares for you?

As you read each of the verses below, consider the reason or benefit the verse gives for trusting in God. Then write it in the space provided.

"God is not a man, so he does not lie. He is not human, so he does not change his mind. Has he ever spoken and failed to act? Has he ever promised and not carried it through?" (Numbers 23:19)

Reason/benefit for putting our trust in God:

_____

_____

_____

"Hope in the Lord; for with the Lord there is unfailing love. His redemption overflows." (Psalm 130:7)

Reason/benefit for putting our trust in God:

_____

_____

_____

"You will keep in perfect peace all who trust in you, all whose thoughts are fixed on you! Trust in the Lord always, for the Lord God is the eternal Rock." (Isaiah 26:3-4)

Reason/benefit for putting our trust in God:

_____

_____

_____

"When doubts filled my mind, your comfort gave me renewed hope and cheer." (Psalm 94:19)

Reason/benefit for putting our trust in God:

_____

_____

_____

"Trust in the Lord with all your heart; do not depend on your own understanding. Seek his will in all you do, and he will show you which path to take." (Proverbs 3:5-6)

Reason/benefit for putting our trust in God:

_____

_____

_____

"Let all that I am wait quietly before God, for my hope is in him. He alone is my rock and my salvation, my fortress where I will not be shaken. My victory and honor come from God alone. He is my refuge, a rock where no enemy can reach me. O my people, trust in him at all times. Pour out your heart to him, for God is our refuge." (Psalm 62:5-8)

Reason/benefit for putting our trust in God:

_____

_____

_____

"God has spoken plainly, and I have heard it many times: Power, O God, belongs to you; unfailing love, O Lord, is yours." (Psalm 62:11-12)

Reason/benefit for putting our trust in God:

_____

_____

_____

"I am the Lord; there is no other God." (Isaiah 45:5)

Reason/benefit for putting our trust in God:

_____

_____

_____

"Jesus told him, 'I am the way, the truth, and the life.'" (John 14:6)

Reason/benefit for putting our trust in God:

_____

_____

_____

God makes it so clear to us. We have every reason to trust him and no reason not to. We're going to take some time to pray and ask God to reveal any people or places we've been trusting in for confidence besides him, so that we can turn our heart toward God instead. There is no rush here! Take some time to listen for God's gentle, encouraging voice. It is filled with love for you.

God,

Only you can see deep into my heart. Please clear out all distractions, and help me hear your voice now. I ask in the name of Jesus that you would reveal any people or place besides you that I've been trusting in for confidence, and help me to put all my trust in you.

This is your free space! If God gives you a picture or word in your mind as you listen for his voice, feel free to draw or write it down here. Remember, there is freedom here! This is just between you and God.

Free Space

God insists that we put our trust in him, because he knows that if we put our trust in people, our looks, or our possessions, we will never have true confidence. God is the only one who never changes and whose opinion of us never changes, no matter what. This brings us to the next key.

Key #2—Live for an Audience of One

Sometimes it feels like, as women, we're hardwired to people-please. We want people to like us. Our desire to gain acceptance and approval isn't bad in and of itself. But God gives us these desires so that he can fulfill them. A problem arises when we look to people to meet needs that only God can fulfill.

If we worry about what others think of us, compare ourselves to them, or try to meet their expectations, we'll be on an emotional roller coaster ride for the rest of our lives, and we'll miss out on the confidence that God has for us. People, as wonderful as they can be, are fickle. But not God. He is our Rock. "Jesus Christ is the same yesterday, today, and forever" (Hebrews 13:8).

One of our favorite Bible stories is about a woman named Mary Magdalene. She was a prostitute who was possessed by seven demons. She was a total outcast from society. She came to Jesus one day, fell at his feet in front of the people he was with, and poured out every last drop of her heart to him. He cast the demons out of her, forgave her for all of her sins, and became her closest friend. Mary Magdalene was one of the few women mentioned as being there when Christ was crucified. And get this, this is our favorite part: Mary Magdalene was the first person to see Jesus after he rose from the dead! Christ chose to appear to her first! Can you believe it? This woman was despised and rejected by so many people, but the Son of God loved her, forgave her, and bestowed the greatest honor on her. Mary's confidence was in Jesus Christ alone. No one else. She cared only about pleasing him. She banked everything on him. And look at what he gave her in return!

Jesus has the same amazing love, acceptance, and honor for each one of us who will come to him, fall at his feet, and pour out our hearts to him, not worried about what others think of us. Read each of the following verses. After each one, pause a moment and let your heart absorb each drop of truth! Then rewrite the verse in your own words, thinking about what the words mean for your life.

> *"It is better to take refuge in the Lord than to trust in people. It is better to take refuge in the Lord than to trust in princes." (Psalm 118:8-9)*

> *"Obviously, I'm not trying to win the approval of people, but of God. If pleasing people were my goal, I would not be Christ's servant."* (Galatians 1:10)

"But the Lord said to Samuel, 'Don't judge by his appearance or height, for I have rejected him. The Lord doesn't see things the way you see them. People judge by outward appearance, but the Lord looks at the heart.'"
(1 Samuel 16:7)

_____

_____

_____

"Pay careful attention to your own work, for then you will get the satisfaction of a job well done, and you won't need to compare yourself to anyone else."
(Galatians 6:4)

_____

_____

_____

"Don't put your confidence in powerful people; there is no help for you there. When they breathe their last, they return to the earth, and all their plans die with them. But joyful are those who have the God of Israel as their helper, whose hope is in the Lord their God." (Psalm 146:3-5)

_____

_____

_____

"But when I am afraid, I will put my trust in you. I praise God for what he has promised. I trust in God, so why should I be afraid? What can mere mortals do to me?" (Psalm 56:3-4)

_____

_____

_____

"Fearing people is a dangerous trap, but trusting the Lord means safety."
(Proverbs 29:25)

_____

_____

_____

"Don't be afraid of those who want to kill your body; they cannot touch your soul. Fear only God, who can destroy both soul and body in hell."
(Matthew 10:28)

_____

_____

_____

God alone has the power to give life and to take it away. Our eternal destiny is in his hands. In the end, we will have no one to answer to except God. It won't matter one lollipop lick how popular we were or what other people thought of us. God sees our hearts, and if we live to please him instead trying to win the approval of other people, we can have true confidence, now and forever. This brings us to our last key.

Key #3—Believe What God Says About You

Girl, we have to level with you. We're still on the confidence journey with Christ. All of us are. No matter how mature we are, how old we get, how wise we become, how whatever—until the day we die, we're going to be on the journey, because true confidence is a daily decision to believe what God says about us instead of what the world says.

The only way to do this is to spend time with Jesus, in the Bible, in conversation with him, taking walks with him, or swims, or whatever adventures we love. He just wants to be with us. That's why Jesus died for our sins. So that we could be with him. He longs for us. He desires us. He loves us just as we are. Only God can give us the confidence we need each day, and he gives it one day at a time.

True confidence is born, nurtured, and cultivated in relationship with Christ, because the more we get to know and experience his love, the more we trust him. The more we trust him, the more we want to please him; and the more we live to please him, the less we compare ourselves to others or worry about what they think of us. The more we are with Jesus, the more we become radically free from fear, anxiety, and insecurity. Because we realize that God made us just the way he wanted us. He thought about the kind of person he wanted to spend the rest of eternity with and then created that person: You.

As women, we crave romance, affection, and adoration. We long to be loved and to belong. God says that if we put our faith in Jesus, we belong to him. No one can snatch us out of his hand or separate us from God's love. Read the following verses, and listen to what God has to say to you. Let God's promises to you make everything else disappear. All fears, all doubts, all insecurities, all failures, all rejection. God desires to whisper to the secret places in your heart that only he can touch.

We've left a little space after each verse in case you want to write any thoughts or a prayer.

"I have loved you, my people, with an everlasting love. With unfailing love I have drawn you to myself." (Jeremiah 31:3)

"Do not be afraid, for I have ransomed you. I have called you by name; you are mine. When you go through deep waters, I will be with you. When you go through rivers of difficulty, you will not drown. When you walk through the fire of oppression, you will not be burned up; the flames will not consume you. For I am the Lord, your God, the Holy One of Israel, your Savior…you are precious to me. You are honored, and I love you." (Isaiah 43:1-3, 4)

"Can a mother forget her nursing child? Can she feel no love for the child she has borne? But even if that were possible, I would not forget you! See, I have written your name on the palms of my hands." (Isaiah 49:15-16)

"I knew you before I formed you in your mother's womb. Before you were born I set you apart and appointed you as my prophet to the nations." (Jeremiah 1:5)

"You are altogether beautiful, my darling, beautiful in every way." (Song of Songs 4:7)

"'For I know the plans I have for you,' says the Lord. 'They are plans for good and not for disaster, to give you a future and a hope.'" (Jeremiah 29:11)

"For we are God's masterpiece. He has created us anew in Christ Jesus, so we can do the good things he planned for us long ago." (Ephesians 2:10)

"For the mountains may move and the hills disappear, but even then my faithful love for you will remain. My covenant of blessing will never be broken," says the Lord, who has mercy on you." (Isaiah 54:10)

"What is the price of five sparrows—two copper coins? Yet God does not forget a single one of them. And the very hairs on your head are all numbered. So don't be afraid; you are more valuable to God than a whole flock of sparrows." (Luke 12:6-7)

The thing that has given me the most confidence in my life, no matter how hectic or hard life gets, is spending time with Jesus. I remember this one day, I was taking a walk around my street to enjoy the fresh air and just be alone with him. I stopped at my favorite view spot for a few minutes, and he reminded me of a verse I love from Psalm 139 and said to me, "My thoughts toward you outnumber the grains of sand on the seashore. I have a whole world of thoughts just for you."

Christie's Story

No matter what happens in our lives, God can give us confidence in the midst of those circumstances. Whether it's a physical wound, an emotional hardship, crazy thoughts that we struggle with, a broken relationship with someone we care about, whatever it is, God will carry us through it and use it for good if we put our trust in him. That's what confidence is all about.

Let's close with four more verses. Memorize the first one! God can transform our deepest insecurities and our darkest experiences into diamonds of confidence.

"Nothing is impossible with God." (Luke 1:37)

_____

_____

_____

"I still belong to you; you hold my right hand. You guide me with your counsel, leading me to a glorious destiny. Whom have I in heaven but you? I desire you more than anything on earth. My health may fail, and my spirit may grow weak, but God remains the strength of my heart; he is mine forever." (Psalm 73:23-26)

_____

_____

_____

"God is our refuge and strength, always ready to help in times of trouble. So we will not fear when earthquakes come and the mountains crumble into the sea." (Psalm 46:1-2)

_____

_____

_____

"And I am convinced that nothing can ever separate us from God's love. Neither death nor life, neither angels nor demons, neither our fears for today nor our worries about tomorrow—not even the powers of hell can separate us from God's love." (Romans 8:38)

_____

_____

_____

TWO: *Three Keys to True Confidence*

Group Study

Settle In and Catch Up
Take 10 to 15 minutes to mingle, chat, and get settled in. Open in prayer, thanking God for this time to be together and inviting God to direct the conversation and fellowship.

Recap
Discuss this past week's lesson. What resonated with you? What did God teach you?

Sharing and Discussion
- Discuss the world's definition of confidence compared to God's.

- What role do you think humility plays in true, righteous confidence?

- What verses from this study encouraged you most? Share why.

Activity—Ingredients for Confidence
Get a large piece of butcher paper or cardboard. Draw a vertical line down the middle. On the top left-hand side, write: "The world's recipe for confidence." On the top right-hand side, write: "God's recipe for confidence."

Have everyone reflect for a moment on what they've studied this week and then call out ingredients the world gives us for confidence. Once you have a comprehensive list, call out ingredients God gives us for confidence. Compare the lists, and discuss:

- Which ingredients are you putting into your life?

- How can we be more involved daily in choosing the ingredients God provides?

Prayer

Read this verse: "My grace is sufficient for you, for my power is made perfect in weakness" (2 Corinthians 12:9).

Get into groups of no more than three. Invite each girl to share an area of her life that she wants God's power to be made perfect in her weakness. Invite everyone to pray for one another in their small groups.

Write prayer requests here: _____

_____

_____

_____

_____

_____

_____

_____

_____

_____

_____

_____

_____

_____

_____

_____

_____

_____

_____

_____

_____

_____

_____

34

THREE: *From Shame to Radiance*

Personal Study

*"Those who look to him for help will be radiant with joy;
no shadow of shame will darken their faces."* (Psalm 34:5)

The Gospel of Luke tells the account of a woman who came to Jesus covered in shame but left radiant. In your Bible, find Luke 7:36-50, and read the story of the sinful woman who anointed Jesus' feet.

- Take some time to reflect on this account. Write your thoughts here.

_____

_____

_____

_____

_____

- When was a time you felt covered in shame? How did you resolve those feelings, or are you still struggling with shame? Feel free to journal about it here.

_____

_____

_____

_____

_____

- What did you learn about Jesus' character from this story?

_____

_____

_____

_____

There are several key truths we can learn from this account in Luke:

- The woman sought Jesus out.
- She trusted Jesus with the ashes of her life.
- She was too ashamed to look Jesus in the eye.
- Jesus wasn't as concerned with her sin as he was with her heart.
- He lifted her shame, forgave her, and covered her with peace and a sense of security.

To experience the ache of shame is to feel inadequate, insufficient, inferior, unworthy, and even unlovable. While guilt is the feeling of doing wrong, shame is the feeling of *being* something wrong. The instant when shame arrives, we are injected with total humiliation and remorse, making us feel naked and exposed. We just want to disappear.

While shame is most noticeably experienced the moment we realize we've done something wrong or stupid or failed to do something right, in its most dangerous form shame can become a pervading experience, shaping our every thought and action.

Shame is costly. Too many of us spend our lives devoid of the security and joy God designed us to be clothed in. Thankfully, whatever the origin, shame does not have to be our destiny.

Throughout most of my adolescence and young adulthood, I wore shame like an uncomfortable undergarment. I knew it was there—closely covering my body, almost suffocating me at times, and affecting the way I felt from day to day. My shame stemmed from a childhood marred by the painful secret of sexual abuse, the betrayal of my stepfather who abused me, and the false belief that it was all my fault.

When we keep a secret such as this hidden, it not only leads to feelings of shame but can also cause us to cope in unhealthy ways. Shame is rooted in the lies we believe about ourselves, and for an abuse survivor, it is especially entrenched in the lie that we are somehow to blame for the abuse. As a result, we are left feeling dirty and afraid of what people would think if they knew the truth.

But just as I tried to keep my secret hidden for years, I also tried to cover up the shame I felt. My outerwear consisted of coping mechanisms such as perfectionism and people-pleasing— anything that would hide my shame from others and instead show them the person I thought they would love and accept.

Shame and anger also caused me to hide from God. I falsely believed he had abandoned me when I needed him the most. But during a season of dark nights, crying and pounding my fists into the pillow, writing in my journal, I found myself asking God to show up and tell me where he was in the midst of my pain.

What I came to understand on my personal healing journey was that God was with me through it all. He was angry when I was angry; he cried when I cried. At times, I even pictured God

Nicole's Story

holding me as a little girl. I read about who he was in the Bible, and in my mind, I could see him weeping over what had been done to me. And the more God seemed to comfort me, the more I wanted to know him.

Through those times of crying out to Jesus in my lowest moments of hurt and despair, I began to understand that God's heart isn't to bring pain or leave us when it gets hard. His heart longs to take the most painful, evil circumstances and turn them into something beautiful. With Jesus as the Author of our stories, we can bring light into darkness, freedom to captives, and radiance to those who felt shame.

I began sharing my story with others and realized I wasn't alone. Telling my secret released me from my past so I could embrace the future. God began freeing me from the pain and shame. Slowly the weight of my stepfather's sin lifted off of my shoulders. Finding the courage to tell put me on a journey to healing, where I discovered the life I'd been longing for. Inviting Jesus closer, I gave him freedom to heal me and use me to make a difference in the lives of others who were once like me: lost and hurting.

I have learned through my own life, and through mentoring other struggling girls, that God meets each of us where we are and extends to us his safe and loving hand. No matter the circumstances in our lives, God wants to enter the story, free and heal us, and use it all for good. He wants us to take a journey with him...a journey from shame to radiance.

The wonderful news is that regardless of where our shame originated, it doesn't have to be our reality. Jesus took the blow for us so we don't have to feel shame. When Jesus died on our behalf, he died for our sin *and* our shame. When we "put to death" or "take off" the nature of our old selves, we can victoriously bury our sense of shame and rise up to live in freedom and radiance.

As we build upon this lesson's theme verse, let's have a closer look at what Psalm 34:5 is saying. What does it mean to be "radiant," and what is it like to be covered with "shame"?

> Nicole Bromley is an international spokesperson on the issues of sexual abuse, rape, and human trafficking. She is the author of *Hush: Moving From Silence to Healing After Childhood Sexual Abuse* and *Breathe: Finding Freedom to Thrive in Relationships After Childhood Sexual Abuse*.

Shame	Radiant
Disgrace	Shining
Dishonor	Bright
Discredit	Luminous
Inadequacy	Resplendent
Loss of respect or esteem	Beaming
Painful feeling of humiliation or distress	Sending out light
	Emanating powerfully from someone or something

Jesus: The Radiance of God's Glory

Have you noticed that shame flourishes where there is darkness? Radiance, however, is the very opposite of darkness. It is a brilliant light or splendor emitted from a luminous body. The idea behind radiance is radiation—not reflection. Any time scientists detect radiation particles or waves, whether it's light from a distant star or X-rays, they know there is a radiating source. The nature or character of that radiation is determined by its original source. In the same way, Jesus teaches us about the character and nature of God. Hebrews 1:3 tells us, "The Son radiates God's own glory and expresses the very character of God, and he sustains everything by the mighty power of his command."

Jesus is both the radiance *and* exact representation of God. Habakkuk 3:4 says "*His* radiance is like the sunlight." Just as the sun's rays teach us about the sun, the radiance of Jesus explains to us who God is. The rays of the sun provide the earth with light and warmth and help make life possible. The Bible tells us that Jesus is the light of the world. John 8:12 says that anyone who follows Jesus "won't have to walk in darkness, because you will have the light that leads to life."

> "*Just as the radiance of the sun reaches this earth, so in Christ the glorious light of God shines in the hearts of men and women.*"[1] (F.F. Bruce)

While it's Jesus who perfectly *radiates* the glory of God, we are to *reflect* his glory to the world. He is the big, true light; we are the little lights. It's like the sun and the moon. We are captivated by the beauty and brightness of a full moon, but really, the moon doesn't have any light of its own. Apart from the sun, it's just a dark, empty rock floating in space. In the same way, without God, we are in darkness. But when we position ourselves in front of the radiance of *the Son*, much like the moon does for the earth, we reflect his light.

We must continually position ourselves in front of his radiance, because just like what happens during an eclipse, there is always the looming threat that the world will get in the way and snuff out our light. A lunar eclipse occurs when the moon passes through the earth's shadow when it is on the far side of the earth from the sun. Our goal as followers of Christ is to continually position ourselves in his light and to keep the world from getting in between us and God.[2]

- What are some practical ways you can "position" yourself in front of the Lord's radiance?

- How does the world sometimes get between you and God?

Contagious Radiance

"Lift up your eyes and look about you…Then you will look and be radiant, your heart will throb and swell with joy…The sun will no more be your light by day, nor will the brightness of the moon shine on you, for the Lord will be your everlasting light, and your God will be your glory." (Isaiah 60:4-5, 19, NIV)

So how do we journey from shame to radiance and move from inadequacy to security?

Allow God to be the lifter of your shame. While Satan is the master shame-artist, Jesus is our shame-lifter. The sinful woman who threw herself at Jesus' feet was not the same when she left. She came to him covered with shame, despair, and disgrace. She left radiant, set free, and new. She was forever changed because she allowed Christ to cleanse her of her insecurity, sins, hurts, and brokenness.

Walk in the assurance that there is no condemnation for those who are in Christ Jesus (Romans 8:1-2). Forgiveness and newness are free gifts from God. 1 John 1:9 promises, "If we confess our sins to him, he is faithful and just to forgive us our sins and to cleanse us from all wickedness."

- What role is shame playing in your life today?

- How have you experienced shame in the past?

_____

_____

_____

- How can you allow God to be the lifter of your shame?

_____

_____

_____

Lift up your eyes. Shame comes from looking inward and outward. A radiant woman looks up to the Lord for the key to life, rather than outward to the world or inward to herself. We can't make ourselves radiant. We have no light of our own. But the more we delight ourselves in the Lord, the more his light overtakes us and consumes our darkness and emptiness. We must make the deliberate choice to position ourselves directly in front of his contagious radiance.

While wreckage from our own sin and unjust experiences such as abuse are two huge sources of shame, it mainly comes from two other sources: what you *look to* and what you *listen to*. Look away from the magazines, the celebrities, the pretty girls. Shut out the noise from the lies you believe.

- What things do you need to stop listening to and looking to in order to experience freedom from shame and inadequacy?

_____

_____

_____

Step into the light. We are called to live in the light (Ephesians 5:8). As we learned from Nicole's story, we experience freedom, forgiveness, and healing when we bring our fears, hurts, and secrets into the light. This doesn't mean that you should broadcast them to the world but that you should be honest before God and a select few trustworthy people in your life. Shame that is spoken loses its power. To be fully known, even for our shameful past or secrets, allows us to be fully loved.

- Are there any fears, questions, experiences, or secrets you need to get off your chest and share with someone safe in order to experience greater freedom and healing?

_____

_____

_____

The Roots of Insecurity

If shame is inadequacy, insecurity is the fuel that breeds its self-destructive fire. An important step to breaking free from the shackles insecurity straps you with is to identify its roots in your life. The sources of insecurity are wide and varied and sometimes hard to pinpoint. We believe that some degree of insecurity is normal, natural, and God-given. At our core, we should know we are weak, insufficient, and flawed. Without a healthy degree of insecurity, we would all be arrogant, self-infatuated narcissists!

"You will know the truth, and the truth will set you free." (John 8:32)

Let's examine some of the most common roots of insecurity:

- Abandonment—being left by a close loved one, such as your mother, father, or an important person in your life.

- Abuse—the scarring experience of being improperly treated by someone. Common forms of abuse are physical, verbal, sexual, and emotional.

- Comparison—the self-destructive and judgmental habit of critiquing other people to determine how you measure up. We most often compare ourselves to other girls or women our own age in the areas we place the most value on. For example, if you personally value the qualities of intelligence or physical attractiveness, it's likely those are the same areas you quickly critique in others.

- Culture/Media—the influences of today's culture (magazines, music, movies, television, and advertising campaigns) that seem to incessantly make us feel as though we fall short of some standard.

- Loss of a Loved One—the incomparable pain of losing a close loved one. Beyond the normal grief process, which often includes feelings of anger, anxiety, hopelessness, and numbness, the effects can be absolutely devastating, forever shaking one's sense of security.

- Rejection—the sting of not being accepted, of feeling betrayed, or getting let down. Experiences of rejection have a way of solidifying the lies we believe about ourselves and keep us feeling as though we're not good enough.

- Self-Absorption, Self-Reliance, and Pride—the excessive fixation on oneself, an all-consuming preoccupation with self. However, it is a lie to mistake insecurity for humility and believe that pride plays no role in one's debilitating sense of inadequacy. Pride can be motivated by our unmet need for self-worth, and pride and insecurity often go hand-in-hand.

- Unbelief—a deep-seated lack of trust; an inability to believe the goodness of God and accept his love for you.

- Do you think there are any other roots of insecurity that we didn't cover? If so, list them below.

_____

_____

_____

In the chart below, check each experience you've felt, reflect on the impact it's had on your life, and write any verses that offer hope and truth. Take time to prayerfully let go of the roots of insecurity in your life.

Root of Insecurity	Your Experience	Your Reflections	Verse/Truth
Abandonment			
Abuse			
Comparison			
Culture/Media			
Loss of a Loved One			
Rejection			
Self-Absorption, Self-Reliance, and Pride			
Unbelief			

Sifting Through the Lies

"Don't get lost in your own head. It can be a dangerous place to wander."
(Allie Marie Smith)

In addition to our sin and life experiences, our thoughts have tremendous power to paralyze us with feelings of unworthiness, shame, and inadequacy. Psychology defines cognitive distortions as "ways that our mind convinces us of something that isn't really true. These inaccurate thoughts are usually used to reinforce negative thinking or emotions—telling ourselves things that sound rational and accurate, but really only serve to keep us feeling bad about ourselves."[3]

While psychology teaches us that it's our own mind that convinces us to believe things that aren't true, Jesus tells us that Satan is the "father of lies" (John 8:44). Sometimes the lies we tell ourselves are of our own making, while other times they come straight from our accuser. The enemy is the master deceiver, who persuades us to believe things that are not true. Satan is sly and subtle. He is the master shame-artist who plants lies in our head. Most often these lies are against us. The enemy disguises blatant lies behind half-truths:

*Your dad left you. You are **unlovable.***

*He sexually abused you. You are **dirty.***

*You aren't model thin. You are **ugly.***

*You still don't have a boyfriend. You are **undesirable.***

Below are a few common types of cognitive distortions.[4] Under each distortion, write your own example of that type of distorted thought you've had.

- All-or-nothing thinking—thinking in black-or-white categories, with no shades of gray. This type of thinking is often rooted in perfectionism and typically includes terms like "never," "always," and "every."

_____

_____

_____

- Mental filter—obsessing on a minute detail and failing to see the big picture. When we over-generalize, we often dismiss positive things and get hung up on a specific concern.

_____

_____

_____

- Disqualifying the positive—dismissing any positive things and only focusing on things we are unhappy or dissatisfied with.

- Jumping to conclusions—drawing conclusions based on little or no evidence. Most often these conclusions are negative and cause us to believe that situations are much worse than they really are. Two of the most common and specific ways we can jump to conclusions are through "mind reading" and "fortune telling." Mind reading is the dangerous art of putting thoughts in people's minds. We've never met a girl who can read people's thoughts, and we doubt you're an exception. Fortune telling is the assumption that future events or experiences are going to occur negatively.

- Magnification and minimization—distorting our own reality in ways that make it seem a lot worse than it really is. It often involves magnifying our flaws and dismissing our strengths.

- "Should" statements—telling yourself you need to be something different than you are. It often involves self-imposed pressure by having rigid set rules or guidelines for yourself by which you judge your sense of worth or accomplishment.

- Personalization—wrongly attributing personal responsibility or blame to situations or experiences. One common thing we personalize is other people's moods or emotions. If someone acts in a way that bothers us, we think it is because of something we did or said.

Renewal of Your Mind

"But you belong to God, my dear children. You have already won a victory over those people, because the Spirit who lives in you is greater than the spirit who lives in the world" (1 John 4:4).

The Bible says in 2 Peter 2:19 that we are slaves to whatever controls us. Too many of us are controlled by the awful things we are saying to our own souls.

Allie's Story

All throughout high school and into college, I was plagued by a never-ending onslaught of self-destructive thoughts. Every night before bed, my mind would replay my interactions from that day. I would mind-read and imagine friends and acquaintances saying hurtful things about me. I would wince with red-hot shame as I thought about how stupid I sounded or foolish I looked. Looking back, I see how irrational all these thoughts were. My self-concept was totally distorted, and people were way too busy thinking about themselves to think bad thoughts about me.

Until we learn to control our self-deprecating thoughts, they will control us. To step into our true identity and become who we are in Christ, we must have the "mind of Christ" (1 Corinthians 2:16). Paul tells us to take every thought captive and make it obedient to Christ (2 Corinthians 10:5). To take a thought captive is to simply grab hold of it and deal with it as needed before it damages your life.

Here's a simple three-part recipe for renewing the thousands of thoughts we have each day:

1. *Recognize* your thoughts. Take them captive, and identify the lies.

2. *Reject* the lies that are not in alignment with God's truth, and refuse to believe them.

3. *Renew* your thoughts. Refine and rephrase them to reflect God's truth.

The only way we'll ever be able to distinguish the truth from the lies is to immerse ourselves in the Word of God. Here are a few verses to consider.

"Put on all of God's armor so that you will be able to stand firm against all strategies of the devil. For we are not fighting against flesh-and-blood enemies, but against evil rulers and authorities of the unseen world, against mighty powers in this dark world, and against evil spirits in the heavenly places." (Ephesians 6:11-12)

"Don't copy the behavior and customs of this world, but let God transform you into a new person by changing the way you think. Then you will learn to know God's will for you, which is good and pleasing and perfect." (Romans 12:2)

- What are some practical ways you can change the way you think?

_____

_____

_____

Meditate on this verse.

"Let your light shine for all to see. For the glory of the Lord rises to shine on you. Darkness as black as night covers all the nations of the earth, but the glory of the Lord rises and appears over you." (Isaiah 60:1-2)

- What is it saying about the nature of Jesus?

_____

_____

_____

Loving Father,
I ask that you be the lifter of my shame. Help me to turn my eyes away from the painful experiences of my past. Help me to release the shackles of insecurity as I believe what you have said about me is true.

THREE: *From Shame to Radiance*
Group Study

Settle In and Catch Up
Set aside 15 minutes to catch up on life before you dig into this week's study. Get to know each other better!

Recap
Discuss this past week's lesson. What resonated with you? What did God teach you?

Lifting Our Shame
As you move into this time of deeper sharing, remember that what is shared here is shared in confidence.

Get a heavy object such as a large rock, book, or backpack filled with heavy stuff. It's best if there is one item for every person in your group—but all the items don't have to be the same thing.

Have each person hold her item in her hand, with her arm extended. See how long each person can hold the item—one minute? Two? When anyone is at her breaking point, have her ask someone else to remove the item from her hand, taking away her burden. Continue until each person has had her burden removed. Then discuss:

- How are these burdens like shame? How are they different?
- We were trying to see how long we could lift those heavy burdens. Do you ever try to hold onto shame? Why don't we try to be released from shame more quickly?
- As you reflect on Nicole's story and your own experiences with shame, feel free to share your story with others in this group. This is a safe place!
- What verse from our study this week has been most meaningful as you look for release from the burden of shame?

Radiating God's Light
Light a few candles around the room. If possible, lower the other lights in the room a bit so you can really see the flames shine. Then continue with your discussion, using these questions as your guide.

- Look at the flames of the candles, and say as many words as you can to describe those flames. How are these words similar to the concept of radiance from this lesson?
- Discuss the analogy of the sun and moon. How does this analogy resonate with you personally?
- Share some specific examples of cognitive distortions you struggle with, so that others in this group can pray for you.

Prayer

Gather around the lit candles; thank God for his light, and for shining that light into our lives. Take time to pray for the specific needs that were shared today. You may want to break into pairs or smaller groups for this time.

Write prayer requests here.

FOUR: *Clothed With Strength and Dignity*

Personal Study

"Anyone who belongs to Christ has become a new person. The old life is gone; a new life has begun."
(2 Corinthians 5:17)

Christie's Story

I've always wanted to look beautiful, be the star of the show, and win the approval of everyone. I've also been the independent type, often headstrong, and a girl who loves adventure. Since kindergarten, I've enjoyed being on stage, curling my hair, and wearing lipstick. I also liked to ride my bike, explore outside, and play detective. I'm unique, just like you.

The thing is, I haven't always felt comfortable with myself. For a lot of my life, I've felt like I have to play a part. Do you know what I mean? Kind of like I'm always auditioning for people to like me or approve of me. I've always been hungry for approval, and throughout my life, I've gone to great and even dangerous lengths to get it.

As a teenager, my desire for approval was all-consuming. I thought if I were pretty enough, I would not experience rejection or loneliness. I was hungry for a sense of belonging and thought that I would find it once I looked flawless, became popular, and fell in love with Prince Charming. I believed the lie that only then, all of my hurts from growing up in a broken home would be left behind, and my heart's longing for love and acceptance would be filled.

Because I believed this lie, I was eager to give my heart to the first attractive guy who liked me. He was older, listened to Frank Sinatra, and had a crooked smile that oozed charm. But the romance was short-lived. He dumped me for another girl. Ahhhh, rejection.

After him came a guy who wasn't as charming, but he was popular and he liked me. I was determined to make my fairy tale come true and gave him my virginity. I thought that if we slept together the relationship would last, but it fizzled out.

Then came a guy who said he wanted to take care of me and treat me right and who told me I was beautiful all the time. We dated for the better part of two years. I got pregnant and had an abortion. I was so hard-hearted from sin and so full of pain and anger that I took my own child's life. I knew exactly what I was doing, but I was scared that if I had my baby I would end up alone. Eventually that relationship ended, too. But the destructive cycle continued. I felt insignificant without a boyfriend because I was looking to men for validation.

Five guys later, I was still unmarried, had ended the life of another baby when I was three months pregnant, and was heavily using drugs and alcohol to numb the sad reality of my life and the disappointment I felt. In an effort to win the approval and love of a man, in order to validate myself as a woman, I had nearly taken my own life.

From the outside, I looked beautiful and even appeared confident to many people who didn't know the inner workings of my life. I was tall, skinny, and tan. I was a model, posing for the covers of magazines, dating one of the richest men in California, driving a new car, and wearing expensive clothes. Designer bags were strewn across my house. Designer shoes were stacked high in my closet. I did yoga and Pilates at a fancy athletic club almost five days a week, and I prided myself on looking "perfect," while inside I could barely remember who I was. My sense of worth was at an all-time low, and I masked my insecurity with a "beautiful" facade.

One night, after another failed relationship, I lay in my bed alone and cried. In the quietness of the night, God asked me a question that changed my life.

"What do you want, Christie?" he said. "What is it that you really want?"

I knew the answer. I had known it all along. I wanted love. At that moment I realized that for more than eleven years I had been trying to get it by using my looks and my body to elicit attention and affection, and this is where my methods had gotten me. Rock bottom.

That night I decided that no matter how bad it hurt to heal, I would do it God's way. Clearly, my way wasn't working. I came to Jesus that night—and many nights and days after—as a total mess, a woman broken to her core. No more facades. But Jesus never once gave me a look of disapproval. Never once did he say an unkind word to me. He told me the truth about a lot of things, and he held me while I cried enough tears to make a small ocean. He gave me and he continues to give me the love and approval I have been searching for all my life. The love I need can only be found in him, because he created me to be loved by him. And only his love will do. He made me just the way he wanted me, designed a destiny for me, and gave me talents to use to influence this world for his Kingdom. He is the only one whose stamp of approval matters. And I already have it. No more people-pleasing!

Coming As We Are

While the world won't love you broken, Jesus does. God wants us to come to him confidently and boldly, even in our weakness (Hebrews 4:15-16). We don't need to clean ourselves up beforehand.

The very instant we come to Christ in faith, turning from our old ways and placing our hope in Jesus, we are given a brand new identity. We are no longer the same (2 Corinthians 5:17). What is true of Jesus becomes true of us. However, before we can walk securely in our true identity and live a life reflective of the new creation we are in Christ, there's some serious, deep soul cleansing that needs to take place.

Malachi 3:2 described God as a "refiner's fire." In a sermon based on this verse, John Piper explains this great attribute of God: "He is a refiner's fire, and that makes all the difference. A refiner's fire does not destroy indiscriminately like a forest fire. A refiner's fire does not consume completely like the fire of an incinerator. A refiner's fire refines. It purifies. It melts down the bar of silver or gold, separates out the impurities that ruin its value, burns them up, and leaves the silver and gold intact. He is like a refiner's fire."[1]

> "You used to do these things when your life was still part of this world. But now is the time to get rid of anger, rage, malicious behavior, slander, and dirty language. Don't lie to each other, for you have stripped off your old sinful nature and all its wicked deeds. Put on your new nature, and be renewed as you learn to know your Creator and become like him."
> (Colossians 3:7-10)

The Lord is righteous and holy, and the actions, thoughts, and life of an authentic Christian should be reflective of the very character of Christ. We are born broken and impure. We all fall short of God's standards (Romans 3:23). While the Bible calls us to change for the good, it is God's always-faithful loving-kindness that compels us to *want to* turn away from behaviors, beliefs, relationships, and emotions that are not reflective of a woman of the light.

Once we catch a glimpse of the marvelous identity God has treasured up for us, we'd be crazy to refuse to accept it. It would be like clinging onto a pair of cheap "pleather" boots when a designer store has offered you a gorgeous pair of brand new Italian-made boots in exchange for your fake ones. Like a pair of dirty, stained clothes, we are to take off the nature of our old selves in exchange for something better.

- We are called to put on our new nature and say goodbye to our old desires and ways of living. Read Romans 6:1-14 in your Bible, and write your reflections here:

- What are some behaviors, relationships, or ways of living God is asking you to put aside?

_____

_____

_____

Let's talk to God, who is filled with grace. This prayer is based on Psalm 139:23-24 and Romans 2:4. How cool that we can pray words right from the Bible!

Loving Father,

Search me and know my heart. See if there are any offensive ways in me and create in me a pure heart. Renew my mind and lead me in the way of life. Expose behaviors, relationships, and emotions that are not in alignment with your best for me, and transform me into the woman you have designed me to be. Thank you for your kindness that gives me the desire to want to change.

Let's break things down and check out some key areas of our lives to see if there's some stuff we need to bring to the light. We will benefit from some careful, totally honest self-examination of the following five areas of our lives.

1. Masks (false identities, pretenses, personas, possessions, or positions we hide behind)

   - Using this definition, what masks do you sometimes hide behind or place too much worth in?

_____

_____

_____

2. Beliefs (false beliefs or things we believe about ourselves, others, and our experiences that go against God's Word)

   - What lies do you believe about yourself that are hindering you from being clothed in your true identity?

_____

_____

_____

3. Thoughts (the mental and intellectual dialogue of our minds; the way we mentally process our actions, interactions, experiences, and relationships)

- Examine the nature of your thoughts. Are your thoughts negative or positive, self-obsessed, anxiety-filled, or impure? What's the hidden life of your thoughts like?

----

4. Behaviors

- What behaviors or ways of living do you need to abandon as you seek to be a girl who walks on the road that leads to life?

----

5. Relationships

- Are there any emotionally or spiritually unhealthy relationships in your life that God may be asking you to walk away from?

Putting It Into Action

Look at this list, and circle some things God may be calling *you* to take off as you seek to be clothed in your true identity and live the life of freedom and wholeness God desires for you.

fear ANXIETY false identities insecurity gossip impure thoughts

SHAME GREED materialism

worthlessness bad relationships DESPAIR

drug use LUST ADDICTION overeating

perfectionism ANGER promiscuity bad language

HATRED negative influences laziness self-obsession vanity disordered eating

"But forget all that—it is nothing compared to what I am going to do. For I am about to do something new. See, I have already begun! Do you not see it? I will make a pathway through the wilderness. I will create rivers in the dry wasteland" (Isaiah 43:18-19).

- What does this verse mean to you? How does it relate to clothing yourself in your true identity?

_____

_____

_____

- How can this verse help you as you strive to take off the things you circled?

_____

_____

_____

The Wardrobe of a "Hard-to-Find" Woman

Proverbs 31 speaks about a woman of God who knows who she is. This chapter comes from the sayings of King Lemuel, where he records words of wisdom from his mother. The section we're going to look at is called "Epilogue—A Wife of Noble Character." While there is no evidence she was a real woman, it provides us with wisdom about the character of a woman of strength.

We like to call this Proverbs 31 woman" a "hard-to-find" woman because verse 10 speaks of her, saying, "Who can find a virtuous and capable wife? She is more precious than rubies." In our world today, as it was then, it is not easy to find a girl who knows her value and is living a radically set-apart life.

Let's peer into the spiritual closet of this "hard-to-find" woman and check out her wardrobe—the attributes and qualities she is clothed in, which are reflective of a woman who knows who she is and who she belongs to. Let us seek to emulate her character.

She is clothed in compassion. "She extends a helping hand to the poor and opens her arms to the needy" (Proverbs 31:20). A woman who knows her value lives an outward-focused life. She joyfully accepts her calling to impart value, worth, and kindness to others. Only once we really comprehend the depth of God's love for us and let it fill the empty caverns of our heart can we truly live a life beyond ourselves.

She is clothed in strength. "She is clothed with strength and dignity" (Proverbs 31:25). She is strong because God dwells within in her. Her strength is not her own—the Holy Spirit is alive in her. She will not fall when the day breaks and storms come.

She is clothed in dignity. *Dignity* is defined as "the quality or state of being worthy, honored, or esteemed." The word denotes respect and status. We live in a world that sends conflicting messages about the dignity of women. Female genital mutilation, sex trafficking, and the violation of women's basic human rights are still widespread in many parts of the world, while women in developed countries such as the United States can run for president, pose naked for Playboy without being stoned to death, and own their own businesses.

A woman who is clothed in dignity knows her high stature in Christ and joyfully chooses to act in ways that are consistent with her identity as a daughter of God. Not only is she clothed in dignity herself but is passionately committed to extending dignity to other girls and women. Jesus was a restorer of women's dignity. Throughout the Bible, we see women come to Jesus. He heals the bleeding woman who has been ostracized from society (Mark 5). He rescues the adulterous woman who is about to be stoned to death (John 8:1-30). Jesus repeatedly treats women with respect, even at a time in history when women have no status.

> "But you belong to God, my dear children. You have already won a victory over those people, because the Spirit who lives in you is greater than the spirit who lives in the world." (1 John 4:4)

As we accept the dignity Jesus extends to us, we should be compelled to fight for the injustices other women, children, and individuals experience.

- How has Jesus given you dignity?

_____

_____

_____

- How can you be a woman who extends dignity to other girls and women?

_____

_____

_____

She is clothed in security. "She laughs without fear of the future" (Proverbs 31:25). Some translations say, "She can smile at the future." This woman who knows her value has a stilled soul. She is not anxious or fearful about the future because she knows no matter what harm comes her way, God's got her back. She's secure and safe in the arms of God.

She is clothed in unfading beauty. "Charm is deceptive, and beauty does not last, but a woman who fears the Lord will be greatly praised" (Proverbs 31:30). A hard-to-find girl is beautiful from the inside out. She is not building her life on her outward appearance or banking her worth on how hot she is. She knows that the surest way to a broken and shallow existence is to build a life on her outward appearance. Her inward beauty overshadows her outward beauty. She knows she has been made for so much more and that, though outwardly she is wasting away, inwardly she is becoming ever more lovely (2 Corinthians 4:16). A woman of unfading beauty makes you feel alive, beautiful, known, and loved when you are in her presence, while a woman of worldly beautiful makes you feel less-than, insecure, and inadequate.

- Reflect on a woman in your life who is clothed in unfading beauty. What is it about her that you love the most?

_____

_____

_____

She is clothed in salvation. "When it snows, she has no fear for her household; for all of them are clothed in scarlet" (Proverbs 31:21, NIV). We believe the reference to being "clothed in scarlet" is a symbol—and even a foreshadowing—of being clothed in the blood of Christ, signifying salvation. To be clothed in salvation is to be a child of God. Above all things, a hard-to-find woman is clothed in her core identity as a beloved daughter of God. To truly know and walk in our value, we must be children of God.

The Bible tells us how we become daughters of God. "Yet to all who did receive him, to those who believed in his name, he gave the right to become children of God—children born not of natural descent, nor of human decision or a husband's will, but born of God" (John 1:12-13).

If you're unsure if you're truly a child of God, we invite you to seek out the counsel of a church leader or wise Christian mentor. And if you haven't already, be sure to read and respond to "Father's Love Letter" in the back of this study. There's additional information there about how to begin a personal relationship with Jesus. Our greatest desire for you is that you'll receive, walk in, and know your identity as a daughter of God.

Loving Father,

Thank you for your mercy and grace. Thank you that I can come before you with confidence because you are filled with grace. I ask that you refine me and mold me into more of the woman you have created me to be. Help me to be clothed in my new identity as your daughter.

Free Space

Welcome to your personal creative space. Reflect on Lesson 4 by journaling, making a collage, or doing whatever you'd like to do!

FOUR: *Clothed With Strength and Dignity*

Group Study

Settle In and Catch-Up
Set aside 15 minutes to catch up on life before you dig into this week's study.

Recap
Discuss this past week's lesson. What resonated with you? What did God teach you?

Clothed in Christ
For this activity, you'll use the "paper doll" figures on pages 59 and 60. On the first figure (the one on page 59), write habits, masks, lies, relationships, or qualities that you think God might be asking you to let go of. Consider these carefully. What have you learned in this lesson that you believe God wants you to remove from your life?

On the second figure (on page 60), write out verses, qualities, and attributes that are reflective of your new identity in Christ. Be creative and "clothe" this figure as you see Jesus dressing you in a new identity.

Get with a partner or in a group of three. Share about what you've written on each figure. Remember, this is a time for affirmation, and all that is shared is in confidence.

After you've shared together, tear out the bottom half of page 59, with the figure representing things you need to let go of. Crumple or tear this figure to symbolize your desire to see God remove these things from your life. Keep the other figure, on page 60, in your book as a reminder of how God is making you new and clothing you with his beauty and grace.

Going Deeper Together
During your personal study this week, you spent time reflecting on and journaling about taking off your old nature and putting on the qualities that are reflective of your true identity. Use these questions to go deeper in your sharing.

- How is God refining you? Feel free to share ways that God has refined you as you've walked with him.

_____

_____

- What role does God's kindness play in causing you to want to change?

_____

_____

- What are the common masks you think girls hide behind for a false sense of self?

_____

_____

- What inspired you most about the "wardrobe of a hard-to-find" woman?

_____

_____

Prayer

Divide into groups of two or three, and submit your own personal requests to God in prayer (no need to share requests beforehand—just bring them right to the Lord in the presence of one another).

r along here

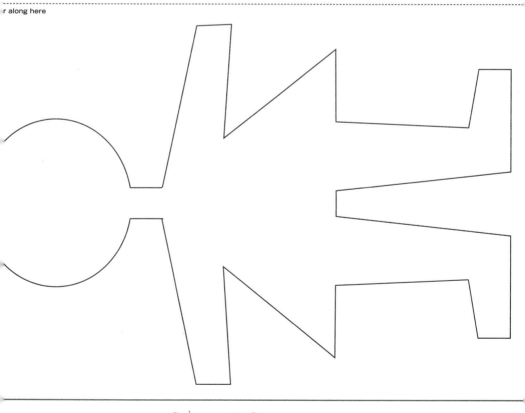

FIVE: *Learning to Live in Freedom and Grace*

Personal Study

"While Jesus calls each of us to a more perfect life, we cannot achieve it on our own...It is only through grace that any of us could dare to hope that we could become more like Christ."[1] (Brennan Manning)

The Plague of Perfectionism

What is perfectionism? According to Merriam-Webster, it is (a) the doctrine that the perfection of moral character constitutes a person's highest good; (b) the theological doctrine that a state of freedom from sin is attainable on earth; and/ or (c) a disposition to regard anything short of perfection as unacceptable.

Sound familiar? If you're like us, you've dealt with this before (or are even dealing with it now)! This section is about moving from perfectionism and achievement-based worth into a life lived in freedom and grace. First things first, let's take a personal inventory.

- Consider the definition of perfectionism above. Which parts of the definition resonate with you? In what ways is your life lived through that lens?

_____

_____

_____

We always want what we don't have—that is, until we have it and we decide that we want something different. We're fickle beings living in a fickle culture. We can't say for sure, but we'd venture a guess that most of you have played the comparison game. You know what we're talking about—you wish you had a body like that girl you just walked by, a job like so-and-so, an exciting life like that girl who always posts exotic travel photos on her Facebook page.

Oh, but I need those shoes!

If only my apartment were bigger.

When I fit into my skinny jeans, then I'll have nothing to complain about.

Even when our lives are going well—we're healthy, we're employed, we have close friendships—we perceive that someone else's life is better, and we decide what we have isn't good enough. *Perceive* is the right word here, because we can never really know what's going on inside anyone else's life but our own. As if anyone would think us more worthy or more interesting if we had a fancy pair of shoes, a swanky apartment, or lost a minuscule amount of weight. Why are we never content with what we have?

As if the temptation to compare ourselves to others wasn't strong enough, the creative mind behind Facebook, Mark Zuckerberg, came around with his social network to take the game up twenty notches. While technology is one of the greatest gifts of the modern world, it can also be one of our greatest enemies. On one hand, e-mail, Facebook, Twitter, and insert-your-favorite-social-network-site-here play major roles in our ability to maintain close relationships with friends and family. On the other hand, these social networks poison our minds with the false belief that others have it better than we do, acting as enablers to our perfectionist mindset.

We read about how delicious someone's lunch was, how perfect their job is, how wonderful their friends and family are. We see online conversations that probably shouldn't be public, and we're so quick to think that our lives are less-than-fabulous in comparison. With each Facebook post and Twitter update, we see nothing but a fragmented image of who these people are, an incomplete (often more perfect) version of their lives that is untrue.

Comparison is a great enemy to our contentment and truly a partner of perfectionist thinking. When we believe perfection is attainable, we quickly and easily fall into the trap of the comparison game. Our ears and eyes are open to all of the ways we could have it better, and we live discontented, dissatisfied lives as a result.

- Can you relate? How has comparison contributed to dissatisfaction in your life?

Singer and songwriter Sheryl Crow had it right when she said, "It's not having what you want, it's wanting what you've got," and she wasn't the first one to talk about it. This idea of true joy coming from contentment is also written about in the Bible, in Paul's letter to the Philippians:

> Not that I was ever in need, for I have learned how to be content with whatever I have. I know how to live on almost nothing or with everything. I have learned the secret of living in every situation, whether it is with a full stomach or empty, with plenty or little. For I can do everything through Christ, who gives me strength. (Philippians 4:11-13)

Simply said (but not always simply done), it's through Jesus that we learn to be content in our current circumstances. It's through his strength that we learn not to want, but rather to see the value in all things we have and in our true identity.

- In what areas of your life are you refusing contentment? Spend some time reflecting, and bring it to the Lord.

You Are More Than Your Accomplishments

Are you an achiever? A go-getter? A list-maker? Do you like to work hard to see the fruit of your labor? Do you feel less valuable and less worthy if you don't accomplish something significant each day?

If you answered "yes" to most of those questions, you might be letting your achievements determine your worth. Don't worry, you're not alone. But you're also not satisfied, are you? It's a weakness that many of us struggle with, making success a god-like figure that we worship.

Deep down, we're trying to earn our value. We're making our own luck, so to speak, and trying to make ourselves worth more. Often we subconsciously do this with God in mind—trying to earn his love and grace through our good performance.

- When have you done something or pursued a goal because you thought you'd be more valuable or lovable once you accomplished it? How did it turn out?

Let's briefly take a look at a few ways we try to be good enough for God through accomplishments.

- The way we eat—Healthy eating is part of living life to the full, something that Jesus himself advocates for us! But sometimes we let healthy eating become virtuous, and we can become self-righteous because we eat well. Why do we choose the food that we do? Are we trying to be good? Or are we honoring our body as God's holy temple by making healthful food choices?

- The way we treat our bodies—We are so cruel to our bodies, girls! We pinch them and poke them and tell them they aren't good enough. It's really unkind, and we need to change our perspective. What's "good enough" when it comes to our bodies? Who determines it? Is it a hard-and-fast rule? Or is it completely subjective?

- The way we serve—Serving others through churches, nonprofits, and our communities is what we're called to do as believers in Christ, but (no surprise here) it's really about the heart. Why do we do what we do? Is it for show because we're trying to earn a pat on the back from God? Or is it an outpouring of service, based on the love we have from Jesus?

- The way we work in school or at our jobs—There's nothing wrong with being a high achiever, but the error lies in the heart's condition. Why do we strive for better grades or more recognition at work? Is it because we want to do our best for God? Or is it because we feel more worthy as a result?

Food cannot make you worthy. Your shape and size cannot make you worthy. Good deeds cannot make you worthy. Grades and accolades cannot make you worthy. Only Jesus can do that, and he says you're worth more than rubies and pearls.

For most of my life, I was a Type-A perfectionist. I was a good girl who did (almost) everything right—I went to church every week, prayed every night, studied hard, went to college, ate healthy, and exercised often. I followed all of the rules because it just seemed to be the way I was wired.

But somewhere along the line, I realized that by following all of the rules, I was doing something wrong. The more I grew in my faith and understood the God of grace, I realized that I refused to fully submit myself to his love. By following rules and living a self-righteously disciplined life, I was missing out on the fullness of the relationship with God that I'd been trying to cultivate.

In time, I surrendered. I realized that God's love and grace could not be earned. I let myself make mistakes. I learned to love and to be loved. I ate foods that were once considered "unsafe" when I was battling an eating disorder, and I abandoned my obsessive daily gym habit. Self-discipline had been ruling my life and shaping my world, and in order to grow, I needed to abandon it and trade it in for beautiful, forgiving grace.

Though grace was what I needed then, I got lost in it over time, using it as license to live as I pleased and not caring for my mind, body, and spirit. The pendulum swung too far in the opposite direction, and freedom turned into bondage. I felt enslaved to my whims and found it impossible to say no to any and all of my desires (food, laziness, you name it)!

Grace can become cheap when it's abused, and discipline can turn into legalism, but true faith walks the line between. I finally see that godly grace and discipline go hand in hand: they are two sides of the same coin, always working to refine and sanctify us into the women we were designed to be.

Discipline honors God, and so does a grateful heart receiving grace. Jesus alone makes us worthy, and no amount of discipline or success can change that.

Natalie's Story

Grace: The Gift That Cannot Be Earned

It's easy to believe that a good and faithful Christian girl should sit back and let God do everything for her; that she should just "be" and rest in the presence of the Lord. And while that is certainly true to an extent, much of Scripture supports God's desire for action on our part. In 2 Peter 1:5-8, we read, "In view of all this, *make every effort* to respond to God's promises. Supplement your faith with a generous provision of moral excellence, and moral excellence with knowledge, and knowledge with self-control, and self-control with patient endurance, and patient endurance with godliness, and godliness with brotherly affection, and brotherly affection with love for everyone. The more you grow like this, the more productive and useful you will be in your knowledge of our Lord Jesus Christ."

Make every effort? Do these things? The image of our proper role gets totally flipped upside down. And that passage is just the beginning. Read these verses.

"Dear friends, you always followed my instructions when I was with you. And now that I am away, it is even more important. **Work hard** *to show the results of your salvation, obeying God with deep reverence and fear. For God is working in you, giving you the desire and the power to do what pleases him."* (Philippians 2:12-13)

*"***Work hard** *so you can present yourself to God and receive his approval.* **Be a good worker,** *one who does not need to be ashamed and who correctly explains the word of truth."* (2 Timothy 2:15)

"Finally, dear brothers and sisters, we urge you in the name of the Lord Jesus to **live in a way** *that pleases God, as we have taught you. You live this way already, and we encourage you to do so even more."* (1 Thessalonians 4:1)

Those places that we highlighted in bold letters are all phrases that indicate action on our part. It's clear that we are called to act a certain way and to pursue certain qualities, but what for? Are we not saved by grace, rather than works? This is a tough concept to wrestle with, but we believe that this is the truth: **God is against earning, not effort.**

Earn: (1) to gain or get in return for one's labor or service; (2) to merit as compensation, as for service; deserve; (3) to acquire through merit.

Effort: (1) exertion of physical or mental power; (2) an earnest or strenuous attempt; (3) something done by exertion or hard work.

By definition, *earning* indicates gain and merit as a result of hard work. If God supported earning, then our salvation and God's pleasure in us would be based on what we accomplish. On the contrary, *effort* refers to exertion and motives. It is not dependent on outcomes or results, but rather on a certain condition of the heart and a desire to do something (for example, to grow in spiritual maturity and knowledge of God).

- In what ways are you trying to earn your salvation? In what ways are you making efforts to grow in faith?

_____

_____

_____

Back in the day, *oxen* and *yoke* were two common terms. Today, not so much! However, let's take a moment to use them in an analogy. A yoke is a piece of wood that connects two oxen, ensuring that they can pull a cart or plow together in unison. One doesn't do all of the work while the other sits back and hangs out; rather, they work together toward their goal. In the same way, God himself invites us to be yoked with him. That's what he means when he says, "Take my yoke upon you. Let me teach you, because I am humble and gentle at heart, and you will find rest for your souls. For my yoke is easy to bear, and the burden I give you is light" (Matthew 11:29-30).

His yoke is easy, not nonexistent. He will guide us, and he will walk with us, but we have to put in some work—some effort! We can never earn salvation, love, or worth; but we can do what is pleasing to the Lord. We can run, we can strive, we can pursue, and with effort we can work together with the Lord to be godly people, effective and productive in our knowledge of Jesus Christ.

The Way Out: Freedom and Grace

Freedom is the quality or state of being free; the absence of necessity, coercion, or constraint in choice or action; liberation from slavery or restraint or from the power of another.

> *So, since we're out from under the old tyranny, does that mean we can live any old way we want? Since we're free in the freedom of God, can we do anything that comes to mind? Hardly. You know well enough from your own experience that **there are some acts of so-called freedom that destroy freedom.** Offer yourselves to sin, for instance, and it's your last free act. But offer yourselves to the ways of God and the freedom never quits. All your lives you've let sin tell you what to do. But thank God you've started listening to a new master, one whose commands set you free to live openly in his freedom. (Romans 6:15-18, The Message)*

Real freedom is not permission to do whatever we want, but rather liberty to choose *not* to do certain things. That's what Paul meant when he wrote, "There are some acts of so-called freedom that destroy freedom." There are certain things we do that feel like freedom—eating too much candy, getting drunk, or being promiscuous, for example—but because of the consequences, we are left in bondage.

- What kind of so-called freedoms are you clinging to?

_____

_____

_____

To live in true freedom and grace, we have to let go, surrender, and fall at the feet of Jesus. We need to recognize that we cannot do anything to make him love us any more or any less. We need to know in our hearts, minds, and souls that we are accepted exactly as we are, and our worth and salvation are dependent not on our own merit, but rather on believing God when he says we are saved by faith. We are accepted by a God that is so enamored with us that he gave his life. To move out of the bondage of perfectionism and performance and into lives rooted in freedom and grace, we need to know Jesus.

> *Perhaps the supreme achievement of the Holy Spirit in the life of ragamuffins is the miraculous movement from self-rejection to self-acceptance. It is not based on therapy or the power of positive thinking; it is anchored in their personal experience of the acceptance of Jesus Christ.*[2] (Brennan Manning)

- You are accepted. Do you believe that? Why or why not?

_____

_____

_____

FIVE: *Learning to Live in Freedom and Grace*
Group Study

Settle In and Catch Up

Spend 10 to 15 minutes catching up with each other and sharing about what's going on in your life this week.

When you're ready, open your Bibles to Romans 12. Have someone read the first two verses aloud:

> And so, dear brothers and sisters, I plead with you to give your bodies to God because of all he has done for you. Let them be a living and holy sacrifice—the kind he will find acceptable. This is truly the way to worship him. Don't copy the behavior and customs of this world, but let God transform you into a new person by changing the way you think. Then you will learn to know God's will for you, which is good and pleasing and perfect.

Next, read 2 Corinthians 12:9-10:

> Each time he said, "My grace is all you need. My power works best in weakness." So now I am glad to boast about my weaknesses, so that the power of Christ can work through me. That's why I take pleasure in my weaknesses, and in the insults, hardships, persecutions, and troubles that I suffer for Christ. For when I am weak, then I am strong.

Take a few minutes to reflect on these verses on your own. Record any thoughts or questions that come to mind; then share with each other.

Jesus Is Better

For this, you'll need two index cards per person (or a sheet of paper cut in half) and pens. Each take your index card or paper and find a comfortable spot to spread out for ten minutes of alone time. On the first index card, write down every accomplishment you're proud of, that's made you feel more worthy or valuable—even the small things, like a good grade on a quiz.

When that card is done, move on to the next. Simply write this:

JESUS IS BETTER.

Come together and discuss:

- What was stirred up inside you while you were thinking and writing?
- Which card will you hold onto? Do you want to cling to your accomplishments or to the loving grace and freedom of Jesus?
- Even if you know the "right" answer, are you tempted to hold onto the other card? Share honestly.

Drop your reject cards in a pile in the center, and then throw them away. If you hold onto the **JESUS IS BETTER** card, keep it somewhere you'll see it every day—like your car or your mirror—so you'll consistently be reminded of the truth that Jesus is better and makes us more valuable than any worldly accomplishment ever can or will.

Sharing Together

During your personal study this week, you spent time reflecting on and journaling about the different ways you've tried to earn your own value through perfectionism and accomplishments. Take turns sharing your responses to each of the following questions:

- How has comparison with others contributed to dissatisfaction in your life?

- In what areas of your life are you refusing contentment?

- When have you done something or pursued a goal because you thought you'd be more valuable or lovable once you accomplished it? How did it turn out?

- In what ways are you trying to earn your salvation?

- In what ways are you making efforts to grow in faith? How can others in this group be an encouragement to you?

Prayer

Divide into groups of two or three, and submit your own personal requests to God in prayer. (No need to share requests beforehand—just bring them right to the Lord in the presence of one another!)

SIX: *Walking in Our True Identity*

Personal Study

"Human nature dictates that most often we will be insecure as we are self-absorbed. The best possible way to keep from getting sucked into the superficial, narcissistic mentality that money, possessions, and sensuality can satisfy and secure us is to deliberately give ourselves to something much greater."[1] (Beth Moore)

Ultimately, knowing our value is not about us. Too many of us are living shallow, fruitless, and inward-focused lives while the world around us hungers for our authentic beauty. God wants us to know our true identity so we will live outward-focused lives as his ambassadors. He wants to fill us up so much that we can't help but overflow.

What the world needs is women who have become awakened to their true value and purpose—because women who really know who they are know they are made for so much more than a pretty, perfect, self-centered life.

There is a glorious adventure, a passionate purpose awaiting those who make the unpopular decision to live beyond themselves. As we lose ourselves in something greater than us, we find the joy and purpose we were created for. We are miserable and insecure to the degree that we are self-absorbed, but we are free to the extent that we are absorbed with Christ and the causes that compel his heart. The more we strive to make ourselves beautiful, intelligent, or desirable, the more self-absorbed and dissatisfied we become. "You will become more beautiful in one day by loving other people than you will in one year trying to get other people to love you. Receive the love you've already been given" (1 John 4:19). Stop striving to get people to love you, and love them.

A New Way to Live

Not only does God give us a new identity, he also gives us a new way to live. We don't have to create a life for ourselves, because when we lose ourselves in Christ, we find the life he's already designed for us. While we have the freedom to make our own choices, such as where we're going to live, what job we want to have, or whom we want to marry, God does provide us with clear, life-giving tips.

It's as if God has filled a blank book of white pages with the outlines of fine drawings. No two books and no two drawings are the same. He hands you a unique coloring book which he's thoughtfully designed specifically for you. He then gives you the freedom to pick the colors and draw on the pages as you wish. When you stay in the lines and choose the best colors for each drawing, a beautiful piece of art results. But if you decide to draw outside the lines, the picture can get confusing—colors blur, the drawing gets fuzzy, and sometimes pages tear. Through the Bible, God has provided us with tips for living, designed for our joy and protection, because of his deep, pervading love for us. What does this new way of living look like?

It leads to life. Read the verse below; then rewrite it in your own words.

> *"You can enter God's Kingdom only through the narrow gate. The highway to hell is broad, and its gate is wide for the many who choose that way. But the gateway to life is very narrow and the road is difficult, and only a few ever find it."* (Matthew 7:13-14)

The narrow road is not easy or popular, and it's never perfect, but it leads to life. It requires self-denial and a killing of our sinful appetites. While the wide road permits us to do whatever we wish—to sleep with whomever we want, to do with our body as we please, and to live as we wish—it leads to a whole lot of drama and plenty of destruction. The narrow road leads to an abundant life which is sure to bring joy, purpose, passion, peace, and ultimately, most importantly, eternal life.

It's bigger than us. Read the verse below; then rewrite it in your own words, personalizing the message.

> *"For we are God's masterpiece. He has created us anew in Christ Jesus, so we can do the good things he planned for us long ago."* (Ephesians 2:10)

As people who've been redeemed, we are God's spiritual masterpiece through the redemptive work Jesus has done on our behalf. Not only is this verse saying we are women of immense dignity but that we are works of art that have been created to do good. We are not idle masterpieces on display for others to look at—we are designed not just to *be* beauty, but to *make* beauty. Not to be served, but to serve. No longer should we live for ourselves, but for God (2 Corinthians 5:15).

It can (and should) be fun. Read below; then rewrite in your own words:

> *"Always be full of joy in the Lord. I say it again—rejoice."* (Philippians 4:4)

Living for God doesn't mean we have to dress ourselves in burlap and sentence ourselves to a solitary life of fasting and silent prayer. The famous question presented in the Westminster Shorter Catechism, "What is our chief purpose in life?" is answered with profound simplicity: *To glorify God, and to enjoy him forever.* Most of us are well aware of the first part of our purpose. But how often do we intentionally enjoy God with total whimsy and absolute abandon? Really, completely, fully *enjoy* God? As we delight ourselves in the Lord, he gives us the desires of our heart (Psalm 37:4). Our heavenly Father is the Creator of every good and perfect gift (James 1:17). Let's give ourselves permission to soak up the fullness of the life we've been given.

It's a life of freedom. Read the verse below; then rewrite it in your own words.

> *"So Christ has truly set us free. Now make sure that you stay free, and don't get tied up again in slavery to the law."* (Galatians 5:1)

Warren Wiersbe has said this: "The freedom that Jesus Christ offers means enjoying fulfillment in the will of God. It means achieving your greatest potential to the glory of God."[2]

Part of God's plan for our becoming who we are in Christ is to allow us to walk in freedom. There are five key things God wants us to experience freedom *from*:

- Freedom from law—Jesus came to set us free from a life of religiosity, perfectionism, and striving. It is only by the gift of grace that we are saved. Instead, we are to be led by God's spirit that resides in us who believe (Galatians 6:16-18).

- Freedom from sin—While the world defines freedom as doing whatever you want and living however you please, we know that this way of living ultimately leads to bondage and destruction. We are to use our freedom not to indulge in our sinful desires, but to serve one another (Galatians 5:13).

- Freedom from pleasing others—We'll never become who we are in Christ if we're too busy living for other people. This doesn't mean we stop caring about others but that we don't have to care what they think of us. We are invited to live for an "audience of one." Though it's frightening to stop caring what others think, it's ultimately fabulously liberating (Galatians 1:10)!

- Freedom from lies—God wants to set us free from the lies we believe—about ourselves, the character of God, and the world we live in (John 8:32).

- Freedom from fear of death—We don't need to be fearful of death, for Christ has overcome it. And one day, we who believe in Jesus will too (1 Corinthians 15:51-55)!

It's a life of eternal significance. Read the verse; then rewrite it in your own words.

> *"Store your treasures in heaven, where moths and rust cannot destroy, and thieves do not break in and steal."* (Matthew 6:20)

_____

_____

_____

We are given the opportunity to live lives of eternal significance and create a legacy that outlasts our time on earth. What a privilege it is to store treasures in heaven.

Walking With God

> *"The Lord has told you what is good, and this is what he requires of you: to do what is right, to love mercy, and to walk humbly with your God."* (Micah 6:8)

As we said earlier in this study, our chief purpose in life is to glorify God and enjoy him forever. He comes near to us as we come near to him, so it's important that we willfully submit ourselves to God—who is all-loving and always has our best interests in mind. Let's now take a few moments to unpack what it looks like to walk with God in the small details and answer the question, "What do we do on a regular basis if we're committed to living for God?"

Pray daily. Even when we don't feel like it, this is absolutely the most important thing we do as women who are living for Christ. Whether we're having a good day or a bad day, we must come boldly and honestly to the feet of Jesus and talk to him. Prayer doesn't mean eloquent words and long monologues but can be as simple as sitting quietly and thinking about God. Don't know what to say? That's okay, too. The Holy Spirit knows our hearts and prays on our behalf when words escape us. All that matters is that we come.

Read Ephesians 6:18:
> *"Pray in the Spirit at all times and on every occasion. Stay alert and be persistent in your prayers for all believers everywhere."*

Submit all thoughts and actions to Christ. This even (and especially) includes the temptation and sin in our lives. Many would agree that honesty is one of the most important factors in a healthy relationship, and the same goes for our relationship with Jesus. No more compartmentalizing allowed, girls! He never makes us feel ashamed or guilty for our thoughts and feelings, and we can safely come to him with all things.

Read 1 Peter 5:7:
"Give all your worries and cares to God, for he cares about you."

Choose love above all else. Gossip, boasting, envy, and self-obsession are all things that happen without effort in our lives. Instead of defaulting to those things in all situations, we should ask ourselves, "What's the most loving thing to do here?" Often, it's probably not what our first instinct would be. We may not know the right answer all the time, but when we walk with God, we ask him to show us what's loving and right and true.

Read Luke 6:32-36:
"If you love only those who love you, why should you get credit for that? Even sinners love those who love them! And if you do good only to those who do good to you, why should you get credit? Even sinners do that much! And if you lend money only to those who can repay you, why should you get credit? Even sinners will lend to other sinners for a full return. Love your enemies! Do good to them. Lend to them without expecting to be repaid. Then your reward from heaven will be very great, and you will truly be acting as children of the Most High, for he is kind to those who are unthankful and wicked. You must be compassionate, just as your Father is compassionate."

Seek the Holy Spirit's power. Ask the Holy Spirit to help us become more kind, generous and others-focused. Like we've said over and over, *we cannot do this thing called life by our own power!* We need something greater than ourselves to help us, and that something greater is the Holy Spirit. When we accept Jesus as our Savior, we receive the Holy Spirit to dwell within us. We no longer are alone to figure out life, but instead have wisdom and power at our fingertips. All we have to do is be faithful and ask to be transformed.

Read Ephesians 3:16-19:
"I pray that from his glorious, unlimited resources he will empower you with inner strength through his Spirit. Then Christ will make his home in your hearts as you trust in him. Your roots will grow down into God's love and keep you strong. And may you have the power to understand, as all God's people should, how wide, how long, how high, and how deep his love is. May you experience the love of Christ, though it is too great to understand fully. Then you will be made complete with all the fullness of life and power that comes from God."

Surround yourself with Christian community. We are created for relationships with others, and we need to continually invest in friends who share our faith and hold us accountable to our new life in Christ. The Christian walk is not a solo race. When life is hard, we need to be carried; when others are struggling, we need to be there to pick them up, too. When we isolate ourselves, the truth can become skewed. Being part of a community of believers ensures that we stay on track and have support.

Read Acts 2:42-47:

> "All the believers devoted themselves to the apostles' teaching, and to fellowship, and to sharing in meals (including the Lord's Supper), and to prayer. A deep sense of awe came over them all, and the apostles performed many miraculous signs and wonders. And all the believers met together in one place and shared everything they had. They sold their property and possessions and shared the money with those in need. They worshiped together at the Temple each day, met in homes for the Lord's Supper, and shared their meals with great joy and generosity—all the while praising God and enjoying the goodwill of all the people. And each day the Lord added to their fellowship those who were being saved."

Remember, living for God cannot be done by our own willpower. Thankfully, when we believe that Jesus is who he says he is, we are given access to the Holy Spirit, who is with us at all times. We can only live for God through the power and strength of the Holy Spirit. We never need to feel alone, abandoned, or fearful, because we have a faithful God who never leaves us or forsakes us. We can walk with God in bold confidence, knowing that we are made worthy by his beautiful grace and love.

A Life of Significance

God invites us to surrender our unique personalities, experiences, abilities, and spiritual gifts to be used so that everyone around us can know his great love for all people. Our individual callings in life are what Frederick Buechner described as the marriage between "world's deep hunger" and our "deep gladness." The truth is, we've been hard-wired to come alive when we give ourselves to something that matters—something bigger than ourselves. But how do we discover what that is? How can we live faithfully in God's will, using our gifts and talents to serve him and the others around us?

Start with these steps:

- Take time to discover the needs, injustices, and "deep hungers" of the world that stir up passion in your heart.

- Examine the things that make you come alive and that you love doing. Keep in mind that you will experience the most fulfillment when you apply the unique talents and spiritual abilities God has given you to the area of your heart's desire.

- Take off the self-imposed pressure to find your "perfect calling," and know that God can use you wherever you are as you do all things for his glory. (If you go in the wrong direction, you can trust that he will turn you around!)

Howard Thurman said, "Don't ask what the world needs. Ask what makes you come alive, and go do it. Because what the world needs is people who have come alive."[3] We're not doing the world any favors by living mediocre lives. It's mutually beneficial that we do what we are created to do—for us and those we serve.

- What makes you come alive?

_____

_____

_____

Another essential piece of living lives of significance is that we dream big dreams and surrender the desires of our hearts to God. As Amy Wilson-Carmichael said, "It is a safe thing to trust him to fulfill the desires which he creates."[4] Dream big dreams, and surrender the desires of your heart to God. When we surrender our dreams and desires to God with the pure motive of exalting him and not ourselves, he is faithful to open the doors.

- Reflect on your dreams and the desires of your heart, and record them below. What are some things that are holding you back from fully serving God?

_____

_____

_____

Surrendering Ashes for Beauty

It's often the ugly bits and pieces of our lives—the things the world tells us we should hide—that have the potential to be used by God in ways you could never imagine. The continual trading of ashes for beauty is a miracle God performs day after day in the lives of surrendered souls. God promises that he can take a chapter of your life that is shameful, broken, or painful and mend it into something beautiful.

> "And we know that God causes everything to work together for the good of those who love God and are called according to his purpose for them."
> (Romans 8:28)

As we receive the comfort and hope that comes from God, we are called to share with others the same comfort we received. This high calling offers others hope in the midst of their own suffering, while allowing your past suffering to be used for good. God can use you radically in the areas in which you've been the most wounded and then touched by his healing.

"But then I will win her back once again. I will lead her into the desert and speak tenderly to her there. I will return her vineyards to her and transform the Valley of Trouble into a gateway of hope." (Hosea 2:14-15)

- What in your life represents the "Valley of Trouble," your place of shame, brokenness, or pain?

_____

_____

_____

- How do you think God may be able to turn this part of your life into a "gateway of hope" for others?

_____

_____

_____

Becoming Who You Are in Christ

As we approach the end of this study, we want to take some time to reflect on the truths that have been tough over the last six sessions. Discovering who we are in Christ requires us to be rooted with the following.

1. **Know the One who created you.** Understanding our true identity starts with knowing who God is. We must explore, pray, ask, and seek. Even when we know that we are God's little girls, the journey of knowing him deeper never ends. Want to know who you really are? Start by getting to know the One who made you.

2. **Be confident, knowing you are free and loved by Christ.** In lesson 2 we learned the three keys to confidence: trust God, stop people-pleasing, and believe what God says about us. Real confidence comes when we understand the depth of our freedom, as well as the unfathomable love God has for each and every one of us. When those truths settle deep within the core of our being, we can't help but live confidently for Christ.

3. **Look to Jesus for true beauty and radiance.** Psalm 34 tells us that "those who look to him are radiant; their faces are never covered with shame," and the truth is simple: we can't make ourselves radiant by our own effort. Instead, we need something bigger and brighter than ourselves (Jesus) to make us shine like a candle in a dark room. The longer we bask in his presence, the more his light will consume our darkness.

4. **Clothe yourself with strength and dignity.** In becoming who we are in Christ, we need to exchange the nature of our old selves for something better. The best part is, we don't have to do the dirty work. We simply come as we are to the feet of Jesus, and he washes us clean. Through bringing ourselves to Christ daily, we let *him* clothe us with strength and dignity.

5. **Live in freedom and grace.** Lesson 5 uncovered the bondage that perfectionism and accomplishment-based worth leaves us in. Now we understand that no longer do we need to earn our worth through looking the right way or doing all the right things. In Christ we've been given the gift of grace and true freedom. We cannot be great on our own, but only through the loving power of the Holy Spirit moving in our lives.

6. **Let your life's work be an outpouring of your faith and true identity.** Lastly, lesson 6 has taught that all of this identity business is about more than just us. Yes, we need to know who we are and what we're living for; but through discovering our true identity in Christ, we also will lead lives that are outpourings of that identity. Everything we do will be done with more purpose and a greater impact. For all of us who know our value comes from Christ, the small moments and the big moments alike all serve to glorify him. From the way we interact with strangers to the daily grind of school and work, our faith has opportunities to shine and reach others with the real, life-changing love of Jesus.

- Reflect on the six sessions of this study. Which aspects of becoming who you are in Christ will be the easiest for you? Which will be the most challenging?

We now encourage you to make a list of six resolutions for your life in Christ. Here are some questions to help you create your personal resolutions:

1. How will you make strides to know Christ more deeply?

2. What will you do to find true God-confidence?

3. How will you let Jesus dictate what true beauty and radiance are?

4. How will you live a life clothed with dignity and strength?

5. What will you do to release the bondage of your past and live in grace?

6. How will you live an outward-focused life, rooted in your true identity?

Take plenty of time to think through your resolutions, and write them on page 80. During your next group study, you'll be asked to share these resolutions, as well as sign at the bottom in the presence of your group members.

When you've written your resolutions, take a moment to thank God for that which comes easily, and ask for his strength to help you grow in the tougher areas. Remember, God is always with us and eager to help, no matter who we are or what our pasts look like.

1. I resolve to _____
_____
_____
_____

2. I resolve to _____
_____
_____
_____

3. I resolve to _____
_____
_____
_____

4. I resolve to _____
_____
_____
_____

5. I resolve to _____
_____
_____
_____

6. I resolve to _____
_____
_____
_____

_____   _____
signature   *date*

Free Space

Welcome to your personal creative space. Reflect on Lesson 6 by journaling, making a collage, or doing whatever you'd like to do!

SIX: *Walking in Our True Identity*
Group Study

Settle In and Catch Up

Spend 10 to 15 minutes catching up with each other and sharing about what's going on in your life this week. Then open in prayer.

When you're ready, open your Bibles to Isaiah 61. Have someone read the first three verses aloud. Next, read 2 Corinthians 4:6-7. Reflect on these two verses.

Sharing Together

Discuss these questions together. You may want to get into smaller groups to share more deeply.

- What is one of the best remedies you know of for insecurity?

- What does the "new way of living" God invites us to look like for you personally?

- What is a cause that breaks your heart that you'd like to shine God's light into?

- Based on this study, what have become some of the new desires and dreams of your heart?

We Resolve...

Share the resolutions you wrote for yourself this week on page 80, during your personal study. Once everyone has had a chance to share, sign the resolution page in front of the group as a sign of your commitment to live according to your true identity in Christ.

Prayer

Form groups of two or three, and pray for each other. You're moving forward in a beautiful adventure! Pray for God to continue what he has begun in each person in your group—and thank him for what has been accomplished through this time together.

Write prayer requests here: _____

_____

_____

_____

_____

_____

_____

_____

_____

_____

_____

_____

_____

_____

_____

_____

_____

_____

But Wait! There's More!

Leader Tips

In this final section, we wanted to give you a few extras. Here's where you'll find added info for the leader and our last notes to you, our reader and friend.

Know your group's needs. Assess the needs, schedules, and desires of your group to decide whether you would like to spread the study out over six or twelve weeks. Work together to find the best time and location to meet

Host a "welcome" meeting. Offer a fun and inviting introduction or welcome time for all the girls in your group before you dive into the first session. Get a chance to hang out with one another, read and discuss the introduction, and solidify your group's calendar.

Be rooted. Remain in the Lord, and remember that you can't do anything apart from him (John 15:5). Carve out plenty of time in your daily schedule to spend with the Lord in prayer, solitude, and Bible reading. Make a continuous effort to pray for all those in your group weekly and prepare for each meeting through prayer, thoughtful consideration, and reflection.

What You'll Need

Lesson 1: J.J. Heller's song "True Things." This can be found on iTunes or YouTube. (You'll need to be able to play it out loud for your group.)

Lesson 2: A large piece of oversized paper or cardboard and plenty of markers

Lesson 3: Candles and matches; a heavy object for each person in your group

Lesson 4: Plenty of markers

Lesson 5: Two index cards (or a sheet of paper cut in half) per person

Lesson 6: Plenty of pens to sign and decorate your resolutions

Listen and facilitate. Be a conscious listener, and remember that your role isn't to monopolize the group discussion, but to facilitate discussion among all of the members.

Build community. Consider planning fun events outside of your regular meeting times to help cultivate more community and deeper friendships.

Have discernment. Be sensitive to the physical, emotional, or spiritual needs of the girls and women in your group. If you are concerned about the overall well-being of any of the participants, encourage them to seek counseling and/or pastoral or professional help.

Be prepared. Review each week's group study before you meet together. Read the suggested activities for each week beforehand, and be sure you have the materials or resources you'll need. These activities provide a fun, creative, and experiential element to the study. Check out the box in the margin for a quick overview of the materials you'll need for each session.

Finally, keep in touch and share your stories. We would love to hear how this study has been an encouragement to you and your study group. Visit our website at wonderfullymade.org and e-mail us at info@wonderfullymade.org to share how this study has impacted you. Please invite everyone in your group to do the same, and remember that you are officially a part of the Wonderfully Made community!

Father's Love Letter

My child,
You may not know me,
but I know everything about you.
Psalm 139:1

I know when you sit down and when you rise up.
Psalm 139:2

I am familiar with all your ways.
Psalm 139:3

Even the very hairs on your head are numbered.
Matthew 10:29-31

For you were made in my image.
Genesis 1:27

In me you live and move and have your being.
Acts 17:28

For you are my offspring.
Acts 17:28

I knew you even before you were conceived.
Jeremiah 1:4-5

I chose you when I planned creation.
Ephesians 1:11-12

You were not a mistake,
for all your days are written in my book.
Psalm 139:15-16

I determined the exact time of your birth
and where you would live.
Acts 17:26

You are fearfully and wonderfully made.
Psalm 139:14

I knit you together in your mother's womb.
Psalm 139:13

And brought you forth on the day you were born.
Psalm 71:6

I have been misrepresented
by those who don't know me.
John 8:41-44

I am not distant and angry
but am the complete expression of love.
1 John 4:16

And it is my desire to lavish my love on you.
1 John 3:1

Simply because you are my child
and I am your Father.
1 John 3:1

I offer you more than your earthly father ever could.
Matthew 7:11

For I am the perfect Father.
Matthew 5:48

Every good gift that you receive comes from my hand.
James 1:17

For I am your provider, and I meet all your needs.
Matthew 6:31-33

My plan for your future has always been filled with hope.
Jeremiah 29:11

Because I love you with an everlasting love.
Jeremiah 31:3

My thoughts toward you are as countless
as the sand on the seashore.
Psalms 139:17-18

And I rejoice over you with singing.
Zephaniah 3:17

I will never stop doing good to you.
Jeremiah 32:40

For you are my treasured possession.
Exodus 19:5

I desire to establish you
with all my heart and all my soul.
Jeremiah 32:41

And I want to show you great and marvelous things.
Jeremiah 33:3

If you seek me with all your heart,
you will find me.
Deuteronomy 4:29

Delight in me, and I will give you
the desires of your heart.
Psalm 37:4

For it is I who gave you those desires.
Philippians 2:13

I am able to do more for you
than you could possibly imagine.
Ephesians 3:20

For I am your greatest encourager.
2 Thessalonians 2:16-17

I am also the Father who comforts you
in all your troubles.
2 Corinthians 1:3-4

When you are brokenhearted,
I am close to you.
Psalm 34:18

As a shepherd carries a lamb,
I have carried you close to my heart.
Isaiah 40:11

One day I will wipe away
every tear from your eyes.
Revelation 21:3-4

And I'll take away all the pain
you have suffered on this earth.
Revelation 21:3-4

I am your Father, and I love you
even as I love my Son, Jesus.
John 17:23

For in Jesus, my love for you is revealed.
John 17:26

He is the exact representation of my being.
Hebrews 1:3

He came to demonstrate that I am for you,
not against you.
Romans 8:31

And to tell you that I am not counting your sins.
2 Corinthians 5:18-19

Jesus died so that you and I could be reconciled.
2 Corinthians 5:18-19

His death was the ultimate expression
of my love for you.
1 John 4:10

I gave up everything I loved,
that I might gain your love.
Romans 8:31-32

If you receive the gift of my Son, Jesus,
you receive me.
1 John 2:23

And nothing will ever separate you
from my love again.
Romans 8:38-39

Come home and I'll throw the biggest party
heaven has ever seen.
Luke 15:7

I have always been Father
and will always be Father.
Ephesians 3:14-15

My question is…
Will you be my child?
John 1:12-13

I am waiting for you.
Luke 15:11-32

Love, Your Dad
Almighty God

How Do I Become a Daughter of God?

"But to all who believed him and accepted him, he gave the right to become children of God. They are reborn—not with a physical birth resulting from human passion or plan, but a birth that comes from God." (John 1:12-13)

While many of you have already committed your life to God through faith in Jesus, this study would be in vain without providing everyone who hasn't done so with a clear invitation to make what we believe is the most important decision a person can make.

Going to church, wearing a cross around your neck, or believing God exists does not make you Christian. It's only by acknowledging your need for Jesus and having faith in him that you become his child. So how do you become a Christian?

Understand why you need to be rescued. *Everyone* needs salvation because we have *all* sinned, and our sin separates us from God. Sin is our failure to measure up to God's goodness or holiness and his perfect standards. All of us sin by the things we do, the choices we make, the attitudes we show, and the thoughts we entertain.

"No one is righteous—not even one. No one is truly wise; no one is seeking God. All have turned away; all have become useless. No one does good, not a single one." (Romans 3:10-12)

Understand that the consequence or result of sin is death and that Jesus died to take the penalty for our sins. When we really understand how much our sin grieves God's heart, that it separates us from him, and that we never can make ourselves better on our own, we're ready to accept what God has done for us through Jesus.

"For the wages of sin is death, but the free gift of God is eternal life through Christ Jesus our Lord." (Romans 6:23)

Know that God is reaching out to you. God became a human to reveal his love and character to us and to stand in our place and take the price of sin upon himself so we don't have to. Through Jesus, God provided a way for us to be reconciled to himself. And we don't have to make ourselves perfect— God is reaching out to us exactly as we are.

"But God showed his great love for us by sending Christ to die for us while we were still sinners." (Romans 5:8)

Believe the best news ever! We have been rescued and saved from death and given life forever through faith in Jesus Christ. God has put eternity in our hearts. Our souls crave to live forever (Ecclesiastes 3:11). God gives us the opportunity to receive our heart's desire for eternal life through faith in Jesus.

Believe this truth in your heart and voice it with your mouth to receive the very best gift—salvation.

> "If you confess with your mouth that Jesus is Lord and believe in your heart that God raised him from the dead, you will be saved." (Romans 10:9)

> "Everyone who calls on the name of the Lord will be saved." (Romans 10:13)

Pray! We invite you to take this time to pray to the Lord and profess your faith in Christ and desire to live for him. There's no exact prayer formula—it's not the words that save you, but your faith in Jesus.

Dear God,

I believe that you love me. I know I cannot save myself. I need you in my life. I admit that I fall short of your glory and your perfect standard and am guilty of sin. I ask that you forgive me and renew my heart and life with your presence. Jesus, I believe you are who you say you are; that you conquered death and that nothing will ever separate me from your love. I am placing my trust in you alone, and I accept your gift of eternal life. Thank you for saving me.

If you have prayed this for the first time to accept Christ, feel free to sign your name and the date of your decision. Now share this awesome news about your decision with someone. And know that we'd love to hear from you too!

_____

signature   *date*

Notes

Lesson 1

1. John and Stasi Eldredge, *Captivating: Unveiling the Mystery of a Women's Soul* (Thomas Nelson, Inc. Nashville, Tennessee, 2007) 146. All rights reserved. Reprinted by permission.

2. http://www.dove.ca/en/Article/Surprising-Self-Esteem-Statistics.aspx

3. http://today.msnbc.msn.com/id/29055786/ns/today-books/t/under-pressure-are-teen-girls-facing-too-much/#.Tx9Un2NSQWU

4. Stanley K. Henshaw and Kathryn Kost, "Trends in the characteristics of women obtaining abortions, 1974 to 2004" (Guttmacher Institute, August 2008).

5. http://www.ncvc.org/ncvc/main.aspx?dbName=DocumentViewer&DocumentID=32315

6. http://www.nationaleatingdisorders.org/information-resources/general-information.php#facts-statistics

7. http://today.msnbc.msn.com/id/29055786/ns/today-books/t/under-pressure-are-teen-girls-facing-too-much/#.Tx9Un2NSQWU

8. ibid.

9. http://www.usmagazine.com/celebrity-body/news/jessica-simpson-ive-always-struggled-with-my-body-200948

10. Eugene Lowry. *The Homiletical Plot: The Sermon as Narrative Art Form* (Westminster John Knox Press, 2001).

Lesson 2

1. Leslie Ludy, *Set Apart Femininity: God's Sacred Intent for Every Young Woman* (Harvest House Publishers, August 1, 2008).

Lesson 3

1. F.F. Bruce, *The New International Commentary on the New Testament: The Epistle to the Hebrews* (Wm. B. Eerdmans Publishing Company; Revised edition June 23, 1997).

2. Analogy inspired by a sermon by Britt Merrick: "Jesus: The Radiance of God's Glory." January 13, 2008. (See, e.g., www.channels.com/episodes/12894839). Used with permission.

3. www.psychcentral.com/lib/2009/15-common-cognitive-distortions/

4. http://en.wikipedia.org/wiki/Cognitive_distortion

Lesson 4

1. Copyright 1987 John Piper. Used by permission. www.desiringGod.org./resource-library/sermons/he-is-like-a-refiners-fire.

Lesson 5

1. Brennan Manning, *The Ragamuffin Gospel: Good News for the Bedraggled, Beat-Up, and Burnt Out* (Multnomah Books, June 28, 2005).

2. Ibid.

Lesson 6

1. Beth Moore, *So Long Insecurity: You're Been a Bad Friend to Us* (Tyndale House Publishers, Inc.; First edition, February 2, 2010).

2. Warren W. Wiersbe, *The Bible Exposition Commentary* (Victor Books; Second printing edition June 1989).

3. Mark Nepo, *The Book of Awakening: Having the Life You Want by Being Present to the Life You Have* (Conari Press; Original edition May 31, 2000).

4. Leslie Ludy, *Authentic Beauty: The Shaping Of A Set Apart Young Woman* (Multnomah Books; July 2, 2003).

Notes:

_____

_____

_____

_____

_____

_____

_____

_____

_____

_____

_____

_____

_____

_____

_____

_____

_____

_____

_____

_____

_____

_____

_____

_____

_____

_____

_____

_____

_____

_____

_____